Cabins to Condos

Fading Frontiers

G. R. Cooper

Having the utmost respect and reverence for Nature and the environment, I have unassumingly related to the life, the times, and the writings of Henry David Thoreau

Thoreau's cabin, drawn by his sister, Sophia

Table of Contents

INTRODUCTION 1

HISTORY DICTATES 9

COLORFUL COLORADO 29

BOOM OR BUST 45

FRONTIER FOOLS 63

GROWTH AND CHANGE 79

ECLECTIC ECONOMICS 97

BETTER OR WORSE 115

RICHER OR POORER 133

SICKNESS OR HEALTH 153

TILL LIFE DO US PART 171

Introduction

"By ignorantly repeating the past, we may never reach an optimal future."

— G. R. Cooper

One cold, snowy late winter evening, while sitting in my Colorado mountain log house in front of a crackling fire, with a hot water bottle pressed against my lower back from shoveling snow that day, I got to thinking. I thought about all the wars fought throughout history, mostly over politics, religion, and valuable resources. I thought about how, with the rising levels of terrorism and violence, the world has obviously not learned from its past. With all that in my mind, I contemplated, as written in Scriptures; humanity could quite possibly be on the verge of the predicted final conflict. Like the pioneers and their cabins, the world many of us have long taken for granted was quickly becoming part of a fading frontier.

As we look around the world today, while observing all the sociopolitical and religious dysfunction happening, we can clearly see mainly one-sided disputes, along with the gross wasting of time and resources. It has become apparent that politics and religion have become far too radical for the overall good of society.

1

Concerning religion, truly religious people would have greater love and respect for others, and would not resort to radical, violent acts, let alone the extremes of terrorism. Furthermore, in a more ethical world, we would not be witnessing religious figureheads, business leaders, or politicians resorting to such moral misconduct as we are seeing today. Ethical transgression has obviously been on the rise in recent history.

The world is therefore long past due for serious change. That being the case, like the onset of spring fever after a long cold winter, I believe that with the emergence of a more educated, knowledgeable youth, along with the widespread overthrowing of world corruption, we are witnessing the blossoming of a shift to collective conscience. Lord knows, the day the people of the world begin to shed their religious and political dysfunction, and come together collectively in spiritual unison will truly be a glorious day.

As a fourth-generation Denver-born resident of Colorado, having such roots, I have chosen purposely to use Colorado as somewhat of a backdrop for writing this book. When I first started writing it, I had been operating the aforementioned log structure, located in South Fork, Colorado, as a quaint little bed and breakfast lodge. Though I kept busy, I couldn't seem to do enough business to afford the special high-risk liability insurance required for bed and breakfasts. Additionally, the cost to heat the place during the ski season had also become a financial drain.

There, in my mid-fifties, after working in the mountain resort business for more than thirty years, I was merely trying to make a go of it on my own, doing something I enjoyed. Unfortunately, after nine months of incubating that B&B, that particular entrepreneurial lodge keeping experience ended.

As that chapter of my occupational life closed, and yet another mountain cabin B&B lodge became a thing of the past, a disparaging feeling suddenly came over me. Oddly, I felt as though I had lost a good friend.

Quietly sitting and staring in deep concentration at the embers and flames dancing within the screened, open-door confines of that woodstove, the fire unable to escape, much like the limits of true freedom and happiness in many segments of society today, I realized the world was at a tipping point.

While sitting there facing the warm fire, contemplating and meditating within my own unique sheltered environment, I could plainly see the big picture looming on the horizon. Our society was sinking rapidly in the quicksand of escalating disaster.

Not accounting for the number of *manmade* disasters, such as the reoccurring financial disasters of recessions caused by human greed and corruption, statistics were showing that the number of natural disasters in 2005 were four times those in 1975. This does not suggest that the changing geo-climatic cycles of Nature are fully to blame, but that an expanding population will eventually reach a critical mass, becoming more vulnerable.

With the world population and its appetite for energy, food, and other commodities continuing to grow out of control, without true leadership, so would human degeneracy, decadence, and disaster.

Barring devastating disasters and evil dictators, I realized that unselfish acceptance of diversity, while sharing values and resources with each other through genuine care and respect, rather than prejudice and hate, was the key to achieving world peace. The question haunting me was this: could we get there in time before destroying ourselves in the process?

As for the escalating level of wars going on in and around the Middle East at the time, I wasn't much impressed with the competitive free world's handling of them. Though an argument can be made and it can be claimed that human sufferance at the hand of dictators demanded action, the lust for oil was obviously at the heart of the matter.

Longed for throughout history, seemingly just outside of man's reach, the *true frontier* of genuine peace and prosperity continues to remain elusive, if not forever fading. As a society, we have found ourselves at the crossroads of change, teetering on the edge of entering what would appear to be a formidable future.

While staring despondently through the screen at the confines of the fire, I had the distinct feeling that things, quite possibly, could get much worse in the world before they actually stood to get better. History, I felt, had given humanity more than enough chances to correct itself, and men had been given plenty of time to learn to collaborate in respect with each other, but had failed while clinging to competition rather than cooperation, thus proving our inability to manage ourselves effectively. In that regard, to my apprehension, my own personal problems at the time suddenly seemed to become comparatively insignificant. There were many more important irons in the fire outside of the one I was gazing into. Then and there, I once again, for the second time since Columbine and 9/11, began writing due to world tribulations, as well as my own disenchantments of the directions in which humanity was heading.

Not long after that, I sold the place in South Fork, and ended up in Cañon City, Colorado, where I entered the federal prisons, not as an inmate mind you, but as a teacher. In doing that, I was astounded to learn that there are nearly two and a half million people in prisons in the United States alone.

By either coincidence or fate, the first class I was assigned to teach, as a community college instructor, was a class in human relations. In that respect, I continue to believe education is the ultimate avenue of change. As perhaps a test of effective communication required of a writer and teacher, I realized that if I could get through to these guys, I could get through to anyone.

As I have written in the past, and will continue to do so, much of my writing is devoted to the sociopolitical environment brought about by money and power, mostly because this extreme form of egocentricity, historically, as well as recently, has been a primary cause of suffering and pain throughout the world, and a major obstacle to world peace. The desire and quest for money and power, fame and fortune, therefore can be looked upon as the true fallacy of all fallacies.

Be it professional sports, politics, or big business, it is disheartening how so many unethical people continue to ignore the laws, rules, and regulations set forth by society, to cheat the system when there is fame and fortune involved. So why even have laws, rules and regulations? Because life without them would be merely a free-for-all, which it seems it is quickly becoming.

So, the question remains: given the counteracting power of education, knowledge, and the wisdom that can come from them, will we ever be able to overcome our egotistical desires, rigid opinions, and dreadful fallacies in order to avoid formidable disaster? Perhaps – provided we are able to humble ourselves and become enlightened enough to shed our erroneous beliefs and self-centeredness. With that, this book is about our fading yesterdays, today, and the questions and challenges of what could possibly become a brighter tomorrow.

History Dictates

"History is a race between education and catastrophe."

— H. G. Wells

As history dictates, rich heritages are passed down from generation to generation – so, too, are stubborn cultures. With a certain amount of education, knowledge, and experience of Colorado history, I've spent a good deal of time observing and studying heritage and culture within one of the most intriguing regions found in North America. Colorado is a place where, outside of its unique majestic mountain settings, also represents a parallelism found in the overall aspects of the rest of American history. Frontier life in Colorado, therefore, became a microcosm of a larger historical picture, with many interrelated events to have taken place in and around other parts of America.

~

It all started back in 1803 with Thomas Jefferson as president, when America expanded its boundaries with the Louisiana Purchase of the western frontier. Soon after that, in 1806, is when the first American exploring expedition, commanded by Colonel Zebulon Pike, came across the Great Plains of the Midwest to arrive at the foothills of the Rocky Mountains.

Other than the early Native Americans, and the Spanish or Mexican interests, the region remained mostly unsettled for many decades after that, until one spring, in June of 1858, when the William Green Russell Party from Auraria, Georgia, discovered gold in Denver's South Platte River near Cherry Creek. Ten years earlier, Green had also partaken in the California gold rush of 1848, so he was already an experienced prospector. It was the following summer of 1859, however, when the Colorado Gold Rush really took off.

Prospect riches were found eventually in the mountains west of Denver, Golden, and Boulder, as well as in the South Park area, and even richer finds of gold were later discovered in the Pikes Peak Region further to the south. Albeit, it was when Robert Womack discovered gold in Cripple Creek in 1890, is when the "*last great gold rush*" took place. Cripple Creek (named so due to a cow that fell and broke its leg in the creek) is known as one of the most famous mining areas in the world, and is still being mined today.

Back during the gold rush era, an ounce of gold was worth less than twenty dollars, depending on its purity, and often took days of backbreaking work in a streambed to extract through a process called placer mining. Over time, as the sluice boxes of the placer mines began to play out, the miners started excavating into the mountainsides upstream in search of veins of precious metal that hopefully would lead them to the *mother lode*, as it was referred to (the primary origin and body of rich ore that was feeding the smaller veins).

Additionally, the Colorado Gold Rush is where the term *Fifty-Niners* and the phrase *Pikes Peak or Bust* come from, as hordes of oxen-pulled wagons flocked in mainly from the east with many thousands of folks looking to strike it rich. People wildly exclaimed, *there's gold in them thar hills*, and so the fever set in to inflict the heads of many a fortune seeker. Naturally, with all this going on, the Native Americans in the region weren't that amused.

In 1859, as the gold rush unfolded, the first stagecoach from Kansas arrived in Cherry Creek, whereby the rapid population growth of the gold rush became the catalyst of Colorado becoming a territory in 1861, prior to it becoming the thirty-eighth state in 1876. Before that, there wasn't any real industry to speak of in the region. The Native Americans, mostly Cheyenne and Arapaho, who lived on the western frontier at the time, primarily lived off the land by hunting, but some tribes historically were known to also grow corn, so I suppose we should consider the Native Americans as contributors to the beginnings of American

Agriculture – the literal roots of early frontier life.

In the days of the American frontier, farming and ranching infiltrated the western territory from other parts of the country, as immigration and the migration of settlers took hold across the region. Life was very basic, with little to no technology to speak of. Guns, wagon wheels, and plows were probably on the leading edge of innovation throughout the virgin west at the time.

With the advent of combines, and other farm implements, farming and ranching drastically and forever changed. These modern inventions, for the times, revolutionized the agricultural industry, making it far more efficient and productive, to where more people began migrating westward. Outside of farming itself, with the increasing population, more industries and businesses could then be supported. With that, came Colorado's first real towns and other businesses, along with all the life-sustaining railroads that supported them.

As the railroads progressed west, the *Union Pacific* reached Cheyenne in 1867, and the *Denver Pacific* between Cheyenne and Denver (Colorado's territorial capital), was completed in 1870. That same year, the *Kansas Pacific* also arrived in Denver. Other railroads expanded rapidly across the country, and the *Denver & Rio Grande* (D&RG) extended south from Denver in 1871 to feed the expanding populations of the Pikes Peak Region and Colorado Springs. Under continued fierce competition with each other, the railroads soon reached out with narrow gauge lines to the many mountain mining towns to facilitate the increasing need for transportation and shipping in those areas. Lines such as the Colorado Central Railroad that ran up Clear Creek Canyon out of Golden, along with the D&RG and the Santa Fe Railroad out of the Pikes Peak Region, battled each other west across the rugged mountains. Railroad forgers, such as Otto Mears, David H. Moffat, and Civil War General William Jackson Palmer were a few of the men contributed with bringing the iron horse and its way of civilization in from the Great Plains to sophisticate and tame the Wild West.

With telegraph lines completed in Colorado in the early 1860s, and the first telephones installed in Denver in 1878, communications with the outside world were established. My grandfather, back in the early 1900s, once worked as a telegraph operator for the Railroad, north of Colorado Springs in Palmer Lake – Palmer Lake named after General, William Jackson Palmer, who as mentioned was instrumental in the development of the railroad as well as the founding of Colorado Springs. Growing up in Palmer Lake, I can still remember the original train depot where my grandfather once tapped out his Morse code on the very telegraph keys that I later came across in my grandmothers shed. Prior to that, he had worked as a telegraph operator at the train depot in Pueblo. In the early days, there would have been a round wooden water tower near the depot sitting up on its latticework of timbers. The tower being located alongside the train tracks next to the lake where the coal-fired steam locomotives once stopped to take on water and to let passengers and freight on and off. Steam locomotives operated in Colorado as late as 1959 when diesel engines took their place.

After working for the railroad, my grandfather owned and operated the Glenside General Store there in Palmer Lake, and was known to give food and essentials at times to certain poor and needy townspeople, especially during the Great Depression. I still have the old wooden skis that he used to get to and from the store during deep winter snow storms.

With the railroads reaching Denver and the Pikes Peak Region in the early 1870s, and the last gold rush taking place in the early 1890s, the state's population continued to grow by leaps and bounds. Civilization, with all of its *uncivilized* problems, quickly took hold. Saloons, gambling halls and, yes, even prostitution became thriving businesses for the booming times, especially in and around the mining camps. There, in the latter part of the

1800s and early 1900s, places like Aspen, Black Hawk, Breckenridge, Central City, Cripple Creek, Georgetown, Leadville, Silverton, Silver Plume, and Telluride became some of the most pronounced mining operations and communities found throughout the western territory. The earlier communities were often referred to as *camps* rather than towns because there were usually more tents in the beginning than actual buildings. As time progressed, however, some of these initial mining camps evolved into actual towns with structural frame, as well as brick and mortar buildings. In the more evolved mining towns, on one side of the street might be a dance hall, while on the other side perchance a theater or an opera house, and just down the same main street, maybe a secluded church. Desirable forms of entertainment, amusement, and services were available for all cultural levels that lived in and around these towns. By 1900, Cripple Creek had become the second richest gold camp in the world, next only to South Africa.

In the late 1800s, agriculture and mining had been the primary industries in Colorado. However, as the 19th century was ending, the need for food to feed a growing population in this country began to outweigh the demand for precious metals, allowing the agriculture industry to dominate. Additionally, with the silver crash of 1893 when President Cleveland repealed the Sherman Silver Purchase Act, this drastically reduced the demand for silver to back American currency. With that, the mining industry, save a few limited operations, further faltered, and except for the many remaining ghost towns and relics left behind, all but eventually disappeared.

Fortunately for commerce, at the time that mining was waning, the demand for recreational resorts and vacation spots materialized progressively to at least partially take the place of mining.

Colorado, no doubt, had its share of prime destination attractions and natural beauty to offer, and mining towns, such as Aspen, Breckenridge, and Telluride, eventually discovered new riches and financial prosperity in tourism. Where the mountainsides had once been teeming with mules and miners, and covered with mineshafts and cabins, they were replaced eventually with ski lifts and villages of condominiums serving the adjacent snow-covered mountainside slopes. Some of these dying mining towns had once again come to life. Other mining towns weren't so fortunate, due to their less desirable and inaccessible locations. Those remain today as only romantic ghost towns among the quaking aspen and tall pines below majestic peaks, with eroding slopes and old cabins weathered by the high altitude and harsh elements – evidence of another historic era of yesteryear gone by.

Industry and commerce in the bigger towns along the Front Range below the mountain mining communities, such as Denver, Golden, Colorado Springs, and Colorado City, found themselves also having to adjust to the changing times.

Agriculture was still very much alive, but certain companies within the mining industry attempted adapting to the times in an effort to survive. As some of us professional ski bums and Colorado history buffs can attest, the mining industry produced some golden threads that became woven into yet another industry, the ski industry, as mining stumbled and passed its baton on to the next runner. As a classic example, certain mine tram manufacturers that could no longer make it in their own dying industry, transformed and diversified themselves in an effort to survive. Instead of making *mining trams*, a select few found themselves manufacturing *passenger trams* (commonly called ski lifts) to accommodate a completely new type of industry and lifestyle. Unfortunately, there wasn't enough initial demand for ski lifts in the early days of skiing to keep all of them in business.

Nevertheless, as history evolved, some of these famous mining towns eventually made the transformation to harvesting their riches from white gold (referring to snow) rather than the precious yellow and silver metals. Tourism, to include skiing, became the second largest industry in the state, taking the queen's throne next to king agriculture.

Other businesses, on the heels of agriculture and mining, sprung up and evolved as a part of the industrial transition, including, for example, businesses such as the Adolph Coors Brewing Company in Golden, Colorado. Outside of food, the supply of and the demand for alcohol is one business that has survived the test of time, standing strong among other time-tested products, including tobacco and firearms. Coors was one of the few breweries in the country that survived the period of prohibition from 1920 to 1933, due to their ability to diversify to non-alcoholic beverages and ceramics.

Today, agriculture undeniably still remains king, but queen tourism has been slowly sharing her throne with high technology as Colorado's industries further undergo progressive change. There on the Front Range, lives a new rising and promising industry in high-tech and renewable energy, sprouting up next to the amber fields of hops and grain.

The petroleum industry, as a primary energy source, played a substantial roll in the development of Colorado's history as well, but was put on hold when the oil bust of the early 1980s sent Denver and other parts of the state into economic recession. Having a degree in geology right out of college, I once worked as a mud-logger and well-site geologist back in the late 1970s, prior to the downturn. However, life on an oilrig wasn't exactly my cup of Texas Tea, so I ended up going back to work in the ski industry where young men could spend their time around ski bunnies rather than roughnecks.

Today, with the rising cost of petroleum and energy; oil, natural gas, and renewable energy sources, such as wind and solar, are making new headway. Tourism, though, has still prevailed over the years, with the mountain resorts reaching new plateaus of popularity.

As the ski business grew, Colorado's purple mountain majestic resorts matured to the point where the cost of skiing graduated to a black diamond price tag for the average skier with a blue square wallet. The cost of snowballs and golf balls at mountain resorts was reaching a critical level beyond what the general market could continue to bear. Due to the high cost of management and labor in general, along with the capital outlay required to compete with other major resorts, skiing was having its growing pains. Today, like most American industries, we are seeing a rash of corporate mergers and acquisitions taking place in an effort to survive and maintain competitive positions. Like globs of oil in water, one by one, the larger ones devour the smaller ones. Additionally, employee turnover and affordable housing in the ski industry remain a persistent problem.

In relation to fading family-owned ski areas, family farms are now disappearing in this country at an alarming rate. I could predict the day would come where agriculture, tourism, technology, and energy will all come under the control of a relatively small number of large corporations. Yes, there are large oil companies that now also own large ski resorts. Sadly, like the mining industry, family farms, as well as family-run ski areas, are figuratively joining the ranks of mining in the Colorado ghost towns of yesteryear.

Throughout history, be it world history, American history, or Colorado history, changing industry and the levels of technology have continued to advance. Regardless, no matter how much the planet improves its efficiencies and productivities, due to social, political, and religious unrest, one thing has remained constant: disagreements often turn violent. Lord knows there were disagreements and violence associated with frontier times.

Today, the world remains at odds with itself. Fading frontiers have given way to formidable futures, meaning that people have evolved through history not learning much insofar as how to get along and cooperate with each other for the common good of all.

It was Edmund Burke who warned us, *"Those who don't know history are destined to repeat it."*

Unfortunately, the disagreements continue stubbornly. I say cabins, you say Cabañas. People have been arguing senselessly and selfishly with each other for thousands of years, yet to agree on much of anything. As for the barriers to reaching a state of true peace in the world, differences continue to lead to arguments, which, by primitive human nature, often lead to anger and violence, and as I mentioned in the introduction of the book, war and violence throughout history have proved to be clearly idiotic.

Outside of perhaps cavemen clubbing each other over the head, historically, the first war on record actually took place somewhere around 2700 B.C., nearly 5,000 years ago. The *where*, *who*, or even the *why* doesn't really matter. What *does* matter is that after all this time, and all the wars, obviously, so-called *civilization* still hasn't learned any lessons from it all, despite all the bloodshed. The term *civilization* may have distinct meaning, but even during the frontier days, we experienced the ultimate oxymoron, what was referred to as *Civil War*.

As I have written in the past, there can never be true peace on Earth, or good will among men, until all humankind become better educated and learn to treat each other wisely and with genuine respect. Only then will problems that we fight each other continually over be solved. As I have also previously pointed out: concerning all of the resources that have been wasted throughout history fighting wars, we could have far better used those resources to educate everyone and to resolve the world's problems. In fact, there probably would have been enough left over to pay off all world debts and to conduct all of the research and development ever needed.

Mulishly, however, throughout history, people have continued the same vicious circles and ignorant choices, adversely effecting both present and future generations repeatedly. We never seem to learn.

For what true purpose do we all keep arguing and fighting with each other? Society needs to wise up and stop this destructive vicious cycle, and to concentrate on education and progression, rather than petty differences. It has actually now become a critical choice that people must make for everyone's survival.

If only the eyes of humanity could have fully opened along the historical way, we might have stopped fighting and disrespecting each other long enough not only to see, but more importantly, to understand all the things Nature was attempting to teach us. There, between all the early morning sunrises and late afternoon colorful sunsets, presented before us were brilliant days of sunshine, shedding light on our true mission and purpose in life – *enlightenment.* Few of this land's inhabitants, outside of perhaps the Native Americans, have ever stopped and reflected long enough to even notice, let alone pay homage to Nature as our true source of enlightenment.

If we had been paying attention throughout history, we would have better noted the carefree existence of the soaring hawks and eagles in the afternoon mountain breezes, or the same loftiness of the gulls in the midday sea breezes. In that respect, we would have noted the guiding examples being displayed to us, such as the underlying respect found between wild animals and their natural environments. Even birds of prey somehow instinctively know and respect their own power and ability to soar above all other forms of life. In the same way, other animals, found below them, also know instinctively certain important secrets of their own lives and environments as well. Somehow, the squirrels seem to know when to start gathering and storing nuts for the adverse conditions of an approaching winter. We see this awareness with all species. Obviously, the animals of the wild possess far more natural intuitive sense than we people often do.

Ultimately, the lesson to be learned here is to listen to and always trust our spiritual intuition and deepest gut feelings, provided we possess the natural ability to tap into them; they are never wrong and will not lead us astray.

Steve Jobs, during the 2005 Stanford commencement speech said, *"Your time is limited, so don't waste it living someone else's life. Don't be trapped by dogma – which is living with the results of other people's thinking. Don't let the noise of others' opinions drown out your own inner voice. And most important, have the courage to follow your heart and intuition. They somehow already know what you truly want to become. Everything else is secondary."* Though it may be one of the hardest and most controversial things I have ever pursued in my life, it is that sense of deep intuition that has guided me in my life and as a writer.

With many people, however, the paradox with trusting their intuition is that it is directly related to their level of faith and conviction in spiritualism. Lacking faith, or having the slightest doubt, means we are not in harmony with the spiritual energy that is always accessible and available to guide us through life. The challenge is actually to gain full confidence and faith in our spiritual intuition, because merely perceived intuition without faith is futile and without foundation. It leads us nowhere, except back to where we came from.

While men have been preoccupied at war with each other, the instinctive aspects that wild animals adhere to, and that *we* should be adhering to, have for thousands of years represented a model of knowledge and natural balance to all. People, on the other hand, seemingly have not learned to open their eyes long enough, through all the spattered blood, to observe and heed these natural phenomena.

Unfortunately, throughout history, people have not refrained from primitively fighting, controlling, and attempting selfishly to manipulate each other long enough to sit up and take notice, while fully understanding what it is that Nature has been trying to teach all of us for thousands of years through a collective conscience. Nature has simply been trying to show us that we have the instinctive ability to soar freely with the eagles above all other life forms. If we would only rid ourselves of our fallacies and fears long enough to redirect our attention from our own fictions, to open our eyes, our minds, and our hearts, and see the glorious, natural reality that exists everywhere around us.

Of course, it can be argued that wild animals also attack and kill each other. Yes, having no choice, they most certainly do as a matter of the food chain, since wild animals have to act on instinct while following the evolutionary laws of Nature pertaining to survival of the fittest. They simply do not have the ability to survive otherwise.

People, on the other hand, being above wild animals *due* to intellect, though I wonder at times, have a distinct *choice* in that regard. That is the real difference after all. Considering this, people naturally possess the freedom to *choose* in *any* type of environment. Therefore, we, in fact, can *choose* not to argue or be selfish, not to fight and not to kill, while at the same time maintaining the ability through intellect to not only survive, but also thrive using ingenuity and innovation. When we choose otherwise, we are being naïve, falling back and relying on primitive instincts, like the wild animals, *acting*, as well as *being* less than civilized. People have, or at least *should* have the knowledge and wisdom to be able to choose to not be manipulative, and not to hurt or to kill in order to survive. Carnivorous wild animals, on the other hand, simply do not have that choice. It all comes down to the level of true knowledge and the resulting intelligence and wisdom (enlightenment) that comes from it.

The moral of all this is that people, therefore, have always had the natural ability to put themselves above and beyond animals, rather than acting *like* animals. World peace and paradise on Earth is therefore achievable and not an impossibility. The true paradigm shift needed is that we should be using knowledge *with* each other in *cooperation*, instead of using weapons *against* each other in *competition*. Knowledge, after all, is the most powerful weapon of them all.

We, as a society, have yet to awaken from our slumber, seemingly to have failed the test of time, as well as the well-guided purpose for being here. Intellect has yet to prevail and dominate. Unless we change, as history continues to dictate the present, it will likely stand to continue molding the future. Though men may have learned to fly physically, they have yet to master the ability truly to soar like eagles.

And so it goes as history dictates. Like solitary mountain men living in log cabins, and country women with their free-spirited love of horses, we continue to become and remain, out of habit, what we are so committed and convicted to.

Colorful Colorado

"Colors are the smiles of nature."
— Leigh Hunt

Being born in Denver, Colorado and having deep roots in this part of the Rocky Mountains, I thought it appropriate to mention a few fascinating facts about the colorful land and colorful people of this state, also known as the *Centennial State*:

Colorado has the highest mean elevation of any state, with more than 1,000 peaks rising over 10,000 feet high and 54 towering above 14,000 feet.

The highest vertical mountain climb is not up one of Colorado's Fourteeners, but up the north side of the Black Canyon near Gunnison. Rising 1,700 feet, this sheer rock face is even higher than the famous Diamond on Longs Peak, and was not conquered until 1969.

In 1899, Crested Butte recorded 254 inches of snow near the top of Kebler Pass. That year, snow buried a train near Leadville and left only stove pipes showing above the cabins at many of the mountain towns around

there. Usually, Wolf Creek Pass near Pagosa Springs and South Fork (both being places I've lived) gets the most snow in Colorado.

The Peck House in the little town of Empire, near Berthoud Pass, is Colorado's oldest hotel. It was built in 1859 during the Gold Rush by James Peck. Early guests included President Ulysses S. Grant, among other famous people. Empire is also home to the original Hard Rock Café, built in 1934 to feed local miners.

Leadville, at 10,200 feet elevation, is the highest incorporated town, not only in Colorado, but in the entire United States. It has also had the highest rate of premature babies, with researchers concluding the cause to be the high altitude.

The largest gold nugget found in Colorado weighed 135 ounces, found near Breckenridge in 1887 by miner Tom Broves. The biggest silver nugget weighed 1,840 pounds and was found at an Aspen mine in 1894. Go figure what both nuggets would have been worth at today's prices.

Measuring 52 inches at the widest point, the antlers of an elk shot and killed in 1899 near Crested Butte are still on display at that town's visitor center. In 1961, Boone and

Crockett declared it the largest elk rack ever recorded in history.

No crops are grown in or around the town of Silverton, north of Durango. At 9,318 feet elevation, Silverton's growing season between frosts is only two weeks. San Juan County there is reportedly the only county in the entire United States without a single acre of agricultural land.

About every 40 years, Colorado experiences a drought, according to tree-ring researchers. The worst was in the 1200s. It lasted 25 years and may have been what drove the Native Americans from Mesa Verde. During the Dust Bowl on the eastern plains, one cloud of dust on April 4, 1935, was 1,000 feet high and 200 miles wide. It traveled at 60 miles an hour, suffocated many animals in its path, and damaged the health of people living on Colorado's eastern plains.

Delta, south of Grand Junction, actually gets less rain per year than Tucson, Arizona.

Winds blowing through the Great Sand Dunes near Alamosa create sounds resembling music. That's how Music Pass above the dunes got its name.

Finally, in 1893, Colorado became the second state in the United States to give women the right to vote (Wyoming was the first). You would think the eastern states would have been more progressive, but it took life on the frontier to make men finally realize how strong and intelligent women really were.

Today, Colorado's historic evolution has created one of the most desirable vacation destination locations in the entire world, where tourism has become a thriving business, as well as a primary source of revenue for the state as a whole.

Oddly related to a wide range of things, including tourism, there's an old principle found in the world, if not the universe, called the 80/20 rule. According to this mysterious statistical phenomenon, many of the things we experience are subject to its bizarre influences. You can look at the 80/20 rule from many different aspects. For example, as a form of business, corporations only comprise about 20% of all businesses, but account for about 80% of U.S. business receipts. Another *related* example could be that outside of sleep, hardworking Americans might spend around 80% of their days on the job *in* those corporations, and only about 20% in leisure activities. This correlates with the fact that approximately 80% of our incomes might go toward basic expenses, with the other 20% going to discretionary spending on other things like vacations. Yet another example of the 80/20 rule, related to the use of discretionary income and tourism, would be the situation that if we choose to vacation in places like Las Vegas; for every dollar we risk gambling, we may get only twenty cents of it back – if we're lucky. As the saying goes, *the house always wins*.

Here in Colorado, we have the old mining towns of Black Hawk, Central City, and Cripple Creek, where the same gambling can be experienced. Lord knows I lost a few dollars *up on Cripple Creek* – Black Hawk and Central City too. I'm sure a lot of other risk takers and gamblers can relate. Yet, another example of the 80/20 rule would follow that 20% of people cause 80% of the world's problems. So, if this 80/20 rule truly holds ground, then it's fair to say that conceivably 80% of the population is made up of basically normal people (whatever that is), and that 20% are just a bunch of thorny folks causing problems for everyone else. To be polite (or 'politically correct' as the term goes) we'll just call them "*Difficult People*". To their partial credit, some can be rather *colorful* individuals, making life perhaps more interesting and entertaining for the rest of us (not that the rest of us are anywhere near perfect).

Working in the mountain resort industry for several decades, I can certainly say that I've dealt with more than my fair share of difficult people. Additionally, as you can imagine, I've dealt with a few characters while teaching in the federal prisons as well.

There's been a lot written on the subject of dealing with difficult people, but over the years, through experience, I've come to the conclusion that there are limitations of patience dealing with some of them. Difficult people are just that, *difficult*, usually due to some deep-seated personal problems that were likely developed early-on in their lives. Not to say that people's problems can't be fixed, but some of the chips on their shoulders aren't easily knocked off, even by professional counselors and psychiatrists. Of course, most everyone experiences sour moods from time to time, but at the extreme, many so-called *bad apples* are just inherently angry and can be downright rude – mad at the world, so to speak.

I truly believe that if we as a society can step back in a preventive mode and tackle the root problems that are causing these psychological conditions, then we can take far more concrete actions going forward to head them off at the pass (as they would have said back in the Wild West days). As anyone might guess, much of this prevention has to do with committing ourselves as an advancing civilization to more life-long intense education and training programs. Unfortunately, money and power too often stand in the way of equitable and pervasive education throughout the world. We'll get into that more later.

Meanwhile, as I was saying, over the years, I've ran into more than my share of difficult and colorful people. One difficult person that sticks out in my mind is a man that I encountered while working at Vail. He was actually staying in Aspen but skiing at Vail that day, where he unfortunately got some lift grease on his ski jacket. Well, after being passed around through the ranks of the frontline employees like a hot potato, he finally landed in the management offices of Vail Mountain Operations (more specifically *my* office), where at the time, I was managing mountain operation systems and finance. The cleaners that we frequently used for these situations usually were able to remove the grease completely through a special process, but were unable to accomplish that on this particular occasion. With that dilemma, I ended up spending a good part of the next day on a shopping trip around Vail Village with the man to look for a suitable replacement jacket. After going in and out of every ski shop in Vail Village, and him not being able to find a single jacket that was acceptable to his discriminating taste, he became even more difficult.

Given that added predicament, I couldn't help but to think about another customer relations' story well-known by many of the senior managers that were still at Vail. As that story goes: an original member of the U.S. Army 10th Mountain Division, and one of the early icons of Vail, Sergeant Brown (better known as '*Sarge Brown*'), was dealing with a very difficult woman who had a complaint and who just couldn't be pleased, no matter what he did. After going to all lengths of trying to appease the lady, in a very stern manner, Sarge Brown asked her if she had ever skied at Aspen. She abruptly fired back at him, "*No! Why?*" He then proceeded to tell her, "*Well, perhaps it's about time you did!*" while ushering her out of his office and closing the door in her face.

Though I was a manager in good standing, I didn't quite have the power or clout of Sarge Brown, so I asked the cleaners to give the jacket one more try with extra careful attention. Thankfully, using an extra special cleaning solution and technique, they were able to remove all the stain. Elated, I had one of our guest services people drive all the way from Vail to Aspen that very evening to hand-deliver the jacket to this gentleman in person. Fortunately, he was finally satisfied. In fact, he later sent me a thank you letter for my personal and diligent attention to his problem. All's well that ends well, as they say.

Another *difficult person* that sticks out in my mind was a woman from Houston, Texas that stayed in my B&B there in South Fork. She had booked four nights for her son and herself at my establishment while they were skiing at nearby Wolf Creek Ski Area. I could tell immediately that this woman had her feathers ruffled the minute she walked through the door. She was the type of rigid person that rarely cracks a smile, and her sternness was only exceeded by her lack of personality. Though I tried to joke with her, she had little to no sense of humor and wasn't the least bit friendly in reciprocation of my welcoming wit. Additionally, this single mother had little to no control over her adolescent son accompanying her, or should I say, she was more likely accompanying him.

The first night of their stay, she was attempting to persuade her boy, who was watching a movie on TV, to go to dinner. He kept telling her to wait until the next commercial. Well, this went on throughout the remainder of the movie, until finally the credits appeared. Observing this whole parent/child power struggle, I just stayed out of it. Frankly, if he would have been *my* kid, I would have just gone over, turned the TV off, faced the lad while pointing to the door, exclaiming, *Get your ass in the truck*! She had obviously not only lost control of her son, but also the respect *of* him as well.

Each morning I would go out of my way to ask them if they slept okay, if their accommodations were suitable to their liking, and if they needed anything else, and each time they shallowly indicated to me that everything was fine. However, on the fourth and final day of their stay, they had oddly packed their bags, prior to the mother taking her son up to the ski slopes. I even gave them breakfast to go since they usually had a hard time getting their act together long enough to have breakfast at all. Well, it wasn't long before the mother came back to grab their bags, wanting to settle their bill with me, while giving me some lame excuse that they needed to be in Albuquerque the next morning to catch a plane. I told her that would be fine, but that I would have to charge her for that night whether she used the room or not since she had already committed to it when she made reservations. At that point, the woman just became *more difficult*, insisting that she was simply not going to pay.

I finally just asked her flat out, "*Okay, what's the real problem here.*" That's when she changed her excuse and said that their room was too cold and that she wasn't going to continue staying in a place that was cold. Keep in mind they had already been there three nights, with me asking them repeatedly if everything was acceptable to their liking, and them indicating each time that it was. Additionally, on the first night of their stay, I had checked them in and shown her their room, and had pointed out the control knob on the baseboard heater, as well as the extra blankets on the shelf in the room's closet, neither of which I later discovered had been touched. She said that if I charged her credit card for the fourth night that she would just dispute the charges.

At that point, I again remembered Sarge Brown from Vail, and concluded that she was just a lost cause and not worth the brain damage, so I finally told her that I was not going to charge her for anything beyond the initial deposit. I then showed her to the door and less-than-politely suggested she never come back, and to go bother some other lodge keeper next time, while closing the door in her face. Though I had lost the battle, I felt as though I had at least won the war. In business, when you're the head honcho, dealing with difficult people isn't really so tough.

Not long after that I posted at the front door entryway of the B&B, as well as on my website, the following notice that I had remembered seeing posted at other lodges and cabins there in South Fork: *"**Ya'll are welcome...if you're nice**."* Apparently, those other lodges and cabins must have also dealt with their share of difficult people in the past.

If only Colorado's cabins could speak, I'm sure they'd tell us of some of the most colorful people that we could ever imagine. It was perhaps a bit easier being such an individual back in the frontier days when there was much more land and wide-open spaces than there were people around. For example, back then, there was the legendary cowboy, who preferably spent a good deal of his time with his horse and maybe his faithful dog rather than around other folks – to him, the cows and the coyotes were usually considered better company. Additionally, there were the desperados and bandits who lived on the wild west side of the law, over the edge of ethics. Then there were the trappers and prospectors, who only saw civilization when they came down out of the hills to trade. All these sorts of solitary men, like Thoreau in his cabin on Walden Pond, were legendary *Loners*, as the term goes, who have, for the most part throughout history, been somewhat discriminated against by the rest of so-called *civilized society*. I doubt that any of them, including Thoreau, really cared much about that though. *Each to their own*, as they say.

Over the years, I've been in and out of many a Colorado cabin – lived in a number of them as well. A few of those cabins didn't have running water or bathrooms, but that was just a part of the novelty and challenge of that type of lifestyle I suppose. The first cabins on the frontier hardly had modern conveniences. They were built mostly from logs harvested from the surrounding forests. From those logs, rough-sawn timbers were sometimes produced for windows and doors. Most had log-framed roofs with perhaps hand-split shakes, but some roofs were just covered primitively with pine boughs and dirt, and the floors were oftentimes only the bare ground.

During the Gold Rush and homesteading eras, when mining, farming and ranching claims were filed with the local authorities, the cabins built on them were called *claim cabins*, and were often constructed as good faith testaments upon the property to let others know that claim was taken. If a claim was encroached upon dishonestly by a *claim jumper*, as they were referred to, in those days, justice was swiftly served – for not only claim jumping, but for any deemed serious offense, including cattle rustling and horse theft. Depending on the severity of the crime, vigilantes rendered three primary means of punishment: beating, run out of town (or camp), and hanging. Hence, crime prevention was quite effective back then. With no holds barred, there would be far less crime these days, be it common, violent, organized, or white collar, if the perpetrators knew that the consequences resulted in facing a frontier vigilante lynch mob. Today, there are too many criminal rights and too many lawyers feeding off corrupt legal systems for justice to be so efficiently served. In the current judicial system, as we have observed with certain high-profile cases, one can actually get away with murder.

From primitive cabins of the old ghost towns and gold mines, to those found around ski resorts, you haven't lived unless you've lived that way at least once in your life. It tends to build character, and color.

Within the historic records, many famous people were a vital part of the colorful Colorado frontier. Included were the likes of Katherine Lee Bates, who originated the song *America the Beautiful* while at the summit of Pikes Peak. There was the *Unsinkable Mollie Brown*, who received her fortune from Leadville mining, and who later survived the Titanic. There was Kit Carson, famous mountain man, guide, and military officer, for which the army post *Camp Carson* in Colorado Springs was named. There was Emily Griffith, Denver opportunity educator, who was murdered along with her sister in their Colorado cabin. There was the famous Helen Hunt Jackson, author of *Ramona*. There was also the infamous trio of American inventors: Thomas A. Edison, Nikola Tesla, and George Westinghouse – all credited for the harnessing of electricity. Much of their competitive experimentation was conducted in and around the mining community of Telluride, Colorado in the late 1800s and early 1900s. Then there was Alferd Packer, who during a severe winter in 1873 cannibalized a group of prospectors he was guiding into the San Juan Mountains.

The complete cast of colorful characters is an extensive one, some of whom I've already mentioned or have yet to mention. Two others, nevertheless, stand out in my mind: William Frederick "Buffalo Bill" Cody, and millionaire miner Horace Tabor. Buffalo Bill, a veteran of the Civil War, and Chief of Scouts for the Cavalry during the Plains Wars, though he claimed to have had many frontier occupations, was best known as a buffalo hunter and for his famous Wild West Shows. His grave, a popular tourist attraction, is located atop Lookout Mountain above Golden, Colorado. Horace Tabor, on the other hand, was a prospector, businessman, and politician. Tabor, who became rich from mining, was best known as the silver *Bonanza King* of Leadville, along with his scandalous relationship with Baby Doe, the estranged wife of a Central City gold miner, and whom Tabor eventually left his first wife to marry. In the end, Tabor's entrepreneurial risk-taking eventually brought him from riches back down to reality. After Horace's death, Baby Doe lived the rest of her life as a recluse in the cabin at the Matchless Mine in Leadville, where her frozen body was found in the late winter of 1935.

Finally, you can't talk about Colorful Colorado and colorful people without at least mentioning John Denver. Born on the last day of the year in 1943, south of Colorado, in Roswell, New Mexico, though he wasn't originally from Colorado, he may just as well have been. John Denver was not only a legend of the music business, and an environmental activist, but he, too, became a true legend of Colorado. Aspen, Colorado, made famous by the romance of gold mining and world class skiing, also became the mountain home of John Denver, who lived a good deal of his adult life there when he wasn't traveling around the world on tour or seeking out natural adventures.

I also lived in Aspen one summer while in charge of a project installing ski lifts there, and though I saw certain celebrities at times, I never ran into John Denver. His songs, especially *Rocky Mountain High*, greatly contributed to making Colorado one of the most prime tourism destinations in the world. One of his earlier hits, *Take Me Home, Country Roads*, was certainly one of my favorite songs back in the early 1970s when I was attending Fort Lewis College in Durango. After Denver's fatal experimental airplane accident over Monterey Bay on October 12, 1997, I can't help but to think that though he died while flying out over the ocean shores of California, his spirit still soars with the eagles over the Colorado high country – *Rocky Mountain High*, in Colorful Colorado.

Boom or Bust

"Prosperity discovers vice, adversity discovers virtue."

— Francis Bacon

With the initial town of Denver established in 1858 during the onset of the Colorado Gold Rush (before Colorado was even a territory), by 1860 it had acquired almost five thousand inhabitants.

In 1862, the territorial legislature, while meeting in Denver, originally selected the town of Golden as its capital, prior to selecting Denver as the permanent territorial capital in 1867. Nevertheless, Golden as the initial capital, is where the first public school in Colorado was established. Coincidentally, I graduated from the descendant of that very school, Golden High School, in 1970.

By the 1870s, Denver's population had grown to approximately thirty-five thousand. As Duane Smith (a previous Colorado history professor of mine) described this boom in one of his books; *"Old landmarks disappeared, replaced by brick structures, as a substantial business district and railroad yards emerged where once log cabins and freight wagons had predominated."* Smith further wrote; *"The catalyst for even faster growth came with Leadville's silver."*

By the early 1900s, life remained relatively simple in Denver, compared with some of the more populated parts of the country. Worldwide, railways, airplanes, automobiles, and ocean-liners were destined to become vehicles of convenience and freedom. Man was to be soon headed down a much different, wider, faster, and more efficient path then he had ever traveled before. The horse, as the once primary means of transportation as well as the source of power and the foundation of work, would slowly but surely be put out to pasture. All the horsepower supplied previously by hay and oats would be multiplied many times over with a new form of fuel energy called petroleum. The industrial revolution and modern transportation were right around the corner to create a new, higher quality way of life.

With the industrial era allowing easier access, by the early 1950s, the population of Denver had grown to nearly half a million, almost half the population of the entire State of Colorado at the time. Today, in comparison, the City of Denver itself hasn't actually increased in population all that much since then, but its suburbs and outlying communities have grown immensely, adding to all of Colorado, which now had a still growing population of nearly six million people.

A great deal of the people that added to the increase in population had escaped from many of the overcrowded places east of the Mississippi, like New York City. Personally, I've never been to New York City, and I don't know if that will ever be in the cards for me since it's hardly a priority of mine. I honestly find it somewhat irrational how the entire world seems to revolve around that city. Related to that, as a writer I would have to say that many worthy books never made the New York Times Best Sellers List, and that a number of books that did, probably shouldn't have. That being the case, because of the highbrowed arrogance of many agents and publishers, I suppose I've never really given much credence to the contemporary publishing world, which seems to cater more to celebrity for the sake of sales and profits than the true art and compassion for writing.

Speaking of big cities, though I've known some fairly credible people that came from them, I'm usually not much impressed with big city competitive cultures. Growing up in a small rural town of only about three hundred people, while being the mostly laidback Colorado country boy I was raised to be, not to stereotype by any means, but it seems to me that a lot of the people that I've ever met from densely populated areas tended to be a bit flamboyant. I suppose they may have thought us rural, native Coloradoans to be fairly reserved. Nonetheless, these kinds of personality differences have a tendency to lead to a gross breakdown of communication throughout society. I suppose much of this is due to the diverse surrounding environments that people are exposed to while growing up, but there we have a classic example of the human relations challenges involving the differences and prejudices that exist among dissimilar personalities and cultures – an age-old problem that contributes to the world's inability to find true peace. I'm not sure we'll ever solve that social dilemma; however, with enough education and training in human relations, provided it could be allowed to take precedence throughout our education systems, I believe we could make great strides going forward in that arena.

We also saw cultural prejudices unfold back in the pioneer days when the *"White Man"*, as referred to by the *"Red Man"*, was migrating out west. The Native Americans and the few Mexicans that were already in the area may have hardly tolerated the situation at first, but as they began to perceive a scarcity of land and resources, more intolerance and violence quickly unfolded. Wagon trains, camps, farms, and ranches were being attacked with vengeance, and in due course, as you would expect, retribution resulted. The Battle of Sand

Creek, in late November of 1864, would be a famous historical account of what came from that. There, in the southeastern Colorado Territory, under the command of Colonel John M. Chivington, the Colorado Territory Militia had tracked down and met up with many of the Indians responsible for these hostile *depredations* as they were called. The history books refer to the battle as a *massacre*, with the militia attacking and destroying an Indian village encampment along Sand Creek, and where many Indian women and children were also slaughtered supposedly. However, there are many mostly credible eyewitness accounts on record that dispute the intentional killing of any women and children. Regardless, however, like all wars, many lives were lost on both sides because of certain paradigms and prejudices that lead to violence and killing. Once again, the outcome should have been predictable with the more powerful of the two enemies winning over the other in competition for perceived scarce resources, and once again, as with so many other disputes throughout human history, *competition* overruled *cooperation*.

Today, and in the same region, we see a similar saga unfolding again, with the migration north of many people from other places moving into the country, occupying apartments and condos, and once again there is an overwhelming perception of scarce resources among the restless natives. It's yet to be seen if all these different cultures can come together in peace; however, I won't hold my breath.

As we've seen, forms of transportation had much to do with taming the Wild West. In the early days of automobiles, once called *horseless carriages*, there weren't that many of them in proportion to the number of people and live horses. However, as the decades and centuries passed, there has since come to be so many cars and trucks today that the Colorado Department of Transportation can't seem to keep up with all of the traffic that is demanding new and improved roadways everywhere throughout the state. Due to the expanding population, and America's love affair with the automobile, it follows that highway congestion has become as much a major challenge here in Colorado as elsewhere, especially along the I-25 corridor of the Front Range between Fort Collins and Pueblo.

Additionally, there is I-70, west of Denver, which passes through Idaho Springs and Georgetown (two surviving mining towns from the Colorado Gold Rush days). This particular interstate conveniently feeds many of the major ski resorts and the mountain recreation areas in the state today, and is more than ever having its share of problems keeping up with all of the added traffic.

Of course, life was much less congested and perhaps more predictable back in the early days of prospecting and mining. That was before economic downfalls and world wars came along in the 1900s to relocate the miners from their mine tunnels, shafts, and placer holes into battlefield trenches and foxholes. Instead of gold nuggets, the only precious metals found in these later excavations were the gold wedding bands that tied men to the lives and loved ones that they had been so harshly uprooted and torn away from.

Unlike previous century wars, such as the 1846 to 1848 Mexican-American War, or the 1861 to 1865 Civil War, and the 1898 Spanish-American war, with the advent of the internal combustion engine powering transportation and other machines around the world, world conflict reached a new plateau never before experienced. For most people, there would be no going back to the simpler days on the frontier. Gunfights confined previously to the old West, which took place with the famous six-shooter and the lever-action carbine saddle rifle, had advanced to much bigger and more powerful battlefields with more lethal weapons deployed on a much larger global scale. Massacres using arrows and bullets that once took place on the plains and in the mountains of Colorado between the cowboys and Indians were being waged in a new era of war between foreign countries often divided by vast oceans.

Gold and silver mining, already diminished in America, was all but halted during World War II in order to utilize experienced miners for mining other critically needed minerals, such as iron, lead, aluminum and molybdenum, deemed more important to the war effort. Precious metals once mined, refined, and transported with the aid of coal-fired steam engines during the gold rushes were being replaced by other valuable minerals and another type of engine powered by a different commodity – *Oil* – often referred to as *Black Gold*.

By the way, the first oil well in Colorado was actually drilled near Florence in 1862. Florence is also where much of the gold ore from Cripple Creek and Victor was originally transported by narrow gauge trains for smelting. It also happens to be where the federal prisons I once taught in are located.

Along with all the wars came the boom and development of the industrial era and the one natural resource, that being oil, required to support so many armed forces and so much industry. With this, the oil industry came of age (prior to that, petroleum in the form of kerosene was mostly just used in lamps). Colorado was certainly along for the ride since Colorado was destined to become one of the favored recreational playgrounds of that prosperous industry. The military and the industrial revolution had to be fueled, and America was fortunately sitting on top of some of the largest oil fields of the times.

An unbelievable amount of wealth was eventually drilled and pumped up from the organic remains of plants and animals that lived in prehistoric eras millions of years ago. Because of oil, Texas was ultimately to become an economic source of power, and much of that wealth and power consequently found its way to Denver in the proceeding days of oil exploration.

Even today, after all of the early oil fields in America have mostly given out, giant petroleum companies have their oily fingers gripping the Middle East. I believe the power, greed, and jealousy brought about by the oil industry contributed to the current problems in the Middle East, along with religious wars and terrorism being waged against America and the rest of the free world. Once again, with America at war, many of the less fortunate would have to die or be injured protecting a rich inheritance of wealth produced by the exploitation of people and natural resources.

America and the rest of the free world can come up with all of the noble excuses they want as to why we have our noses planted in the Middle East, but we all should know the *real* reason by now – Black Gold. Don't be fooled or misled to think that the United States ever went overseas and invaded the Middle East to save the people being persecuted by evil dictators. Underneath all the platitude excuses found on the surface, lie rich and powerful resources and industries, bigger than government itself, with corruption and greed putting profits ahead of people. In fact, I believe these corporate entities have become so rich and powerful that they have, in effect, dictated who actually gets elected in Washington, whereby indirectly dictating both domestic and foreign policy as well. By definition of an oligarchy, that would make them a new source of government, so perhaps we should be calling it an oil-igarchy. I don't know about anyone else, but that situation scares the hell out of me. It means that certain giant corporations, through lobbying, have now taken over power and control of the government of the United States of America. Ralph Nader tried to warn us about that happening. It was he who said, *"Like sex in Victorian England, the reality of Big Business today is our big dirty secret."* He also said, *"The corporate lobby in Washington is basically designed to stifle all legislative activity on behalf of consumers."* Ralph Nader, like the boy who cried wolf, was mostly ridiculed and ignored.

Once again, due to the lust for gold, black gold, our sons and daughters were indirectly being sent off to war, mostly to protect the business concerns of certain covetous corporations. When it comes to propping up the dollar and the corporate assets of America, military superiority has since taken over in substitute of the gold and silver standards.

Our military is being deployed to fight and die not so much in the patriotic name of mom, apple pie, and democracy, but primarily to protect resources that produce lucrative fortunes, which mostly flow to the top echelon of our society. Sadly, brave solders are no longer just dying to preserve freedom and democracy, as we have been brainwashed to believe, but they're giving their lives to preserve the affluence of the rich and powerful. Deny it if you must, but the ravenous wolves are upon the Earth, going for the jugular, with oil dripping off their fangs.

With this capitalistic, predatory condition, who is it you're really voting for in national elections these days (not that your vote actually counts all that much anymore)? Now, take a long, hard look at their backgrounds, where they come from, along with their special interests. With the exception of certain young moderates, most are just slick politicians claiming to be acting in the best interest of their constituents, when they're really acting in the best interest of the large organizations that greatly funded their campaigns to get them elected. I would tend to agree with one of my favorite characters from history, Mark Twain, when he said, *"There is no distinctly Native American criminal class...save Congress".*

In principle, back in history, although on a much smaller scale, things weren't all that politically different in the days following the gold and silver rushes, where the wealthy mine owners of the bigger mines dictated a back-breaking way of life for the miners that they employed, or should we say enslaved. Those miners truly ended up owing their souls to the company store, as the ballad goes. They'd been better off as cowboys on the wide-open ranges than enslaved mine workers confined to these claustrophobic hellholes.

Today, the old mines, big or small, found west of Denver and Colorado Springs, have since been replaced by large corporate casinos that mine the gold out of the pockets of people, rather than from pockets of hard rock.

With gold, it requires added elements or alloys for it to become strong and resilient, since pure 24 kt gold is relatively soft. Without these added elements, it's highly susceptible to wearing down. In the same respect, people without the added elements of instilled values and principles, in addition to hope and faith, also wear down more quickly. Thus, historically, the mountains west of Denver and Colorado Springs in the Colorado Rockies wore down many a miner who lost their way. It stands that the same *boom or bust* conditions afflict today's gamblers as well.

I suppose I could be considered a character from both worlds – the past, as well as the present, since my family once owned an old, small gold mine west of Denver in Black Hawk, next to Central City, where I spent time as an adolescent. I can remember once, going into the local hardware store in Golden with my older brother to buy a case of dynamite for the mine. My brother, who met the age requirement for buying dynamite, only needed to show his driver's license and fill out a simple form at the time. Try to purchase a case of dynamite from a local hardware store today.

Black Hawk, back then in the 1960s, was a far cry from what it has become today. Our family mine, originally named the *Billings Mine*, was located up a rough dirt road in Chase Gulch. The only utility available at the time was electricity. There was no running water, outside of the mine tailings contaminated water running in the creek below, so if you wanted to wash up, you had to hike down to the creek to do that. If you wanted the luxury of hot water, you had to haul a bucket of it up the hill to heat it over the old oil-burning stove in the mine building. Potable water had to be hauled in. When Nature called, there was a plain-old outhouse with a door flap made of canvas for privacy and to keep at least some of the cold morning wind out.

Meals were usually eaten between two pieces of bread or out of a can. If you wanted a hot meal, you cooked it over a hot plate or on the same archaic stove used to heat water. Either that or you went into Black Hawk or Central City to eat in one of the few small restaurants and diners there.

I can remember living at the mine one summer after graduating from college with my degree in geology, and going into Black Hawk for a burger and a cold Coors beer on occasion. I would usually just go to a place called *Crook's* there, which incidentally as far as I know is still in operation and known to be the oldest saloon in Colorado. Entertainment in the area at the time, before the casinos came to town, was fairly scarce. So, after finishing my burger and beer, while dodging the rolled-up sidewalks, I would wander back up to the mine to do some reading and maybe listen to the radio before crawling into my sleeping bag on top of a drab, old army cot.

In Black Hawk, today, one can now make reservations for luxury accommodations and fine dining in world-class casino gaming establishments. Ironically, later in life, I once interviewed for a job as a risk manager with one of the largest casinos there in Black Hawk. However, I decided against taking that job, mostly in principle, since I don't really care for casino gambling all that much, and besides, the cigarette and cigar smoke, before it was outlawed in those establishments, was more than I could stand. Risk management and gaming may incongruously go together, but they weren't in the cards, so to speak, for me. No, I think I would prefer to remember historic Black Hawk and Central City the way they used to be, and I feel quite fortunate and humbly proud to be able to claim that I actually worked a *real* gold mine there, before gambling took over.

I have to wonder how and when the mountain ski resorts and gaming establishments will eventually pass *their* batons of commerce in the future. Like the mining industry, will risk management factors, environmental and technological concerns, the cost of producing goods and services, along with the gross separation of scarce labor and excessively expensive management, possibly dictate *their* fate as well? When will the *mother lode vein* actually pinch out? One of the primary principles of business is that all businesses, big or small, eventually reach their maturity. Yes, it may even happen to Walmart one day down the road. Many times, competition or greed and corruption hurry along or accelerate this maturing process. Sometimes it's brought about by economic downfalls and changes in regulations, and sometimes the world just happens to turn and go in another direction. Safe to assume, wherever there is money to be made, self-serving egos are there to make more than their fair share of it. One can just picture the poor miners of yesteryear working their fingers to the bone for next to nothing in compensation while the mine owners and managers were living the high life, *high on the hog*, so to speak. After spending so much of my career in the mountain resort industry, I can attest that the very same thing is going on there as well. The only consolation today is that labor has more government regulations and restrictions protecting them. Most are still working for peanuts in relation to upper management however. In that respect, some things never seem to change.

Unfortunately, for the lower classes, capitalism breeds a level of greed that eventually and inevitably will destroy the very fabric of the society that created it. Look around America today, and you'll observe the slow deterioration of the American dream, a situation that has and will continue to lead our country into grave crises.

With past and pending crises, we now have a major one looming just over the horizon involving the baby boom generation. Instead of *boom* prospects, this situation may likely pan out to be mostly a *bust*. With the baby boomers, we could have a large generation that may quickly become a great burden upon the rest of America if the majority of them retire and become mostly unproductive, causing a financial liability and drain upon the country.

Additionally considering the world's burdens, we continue to see people wasting energy and disregarding all warnings of global warming. Either they believe that global warming is just a fluke, or perhaps they've just become indifferent to it. I think it's more a case of the latter, with certain people in the free world doing whatever they want, whenever they want, however they want, just because they could. That is, as long as they could still afford to, all of which I suppose is subject to voluntary or involuntary change. Hopefully, the upcoming generations will discover new technologies along with forms of energy and transportation that are more conservative, carbon neutral, and environmentally friendly.

In the same light, it's discouraging to go around the house replacing traditional light bulbs with the new energy-efficient ones, only to see so much of the country continuing to waste energy. Back in the frontier days, before there were light bulbs of any kind, people were more naturally frugal. Prior to Denver obtaining electric lights in 1883, back then, unless there was a full moon, the town became mostly dark come nightfall – by day there was sunlight, and by night mere lamplight.

As with the passing of the western frontier where primitive cabins were replaced by more sophisticated frame and brick structures, so too went the passing of the industrial era as manufacturing was being outsourced to other countries that had cheaper labor. Consequently, many factories in America became part of what was referred to as the *Rust Belt*, and like the dying mining industry (converting cabins to condos), many of these factories were also being converted to contemporary condominiums.

We have now come full circle, from the early gold rush days of prospecting for precious metals, to the industrial era of prospecting for black gold, to the world's present growing lust for fortune gambling once again. After reaching the peak of precious metal and oil production, and with the supply of these resources beginning to run out due to insatiable world demand, we are now drilling farther offshore and back digging deeper within the mines. Yes, with world population expanding, and valuable resources diminishing, we have indeed come full circle to find ourselves in yet another booming gold rush.

Be it precious metals or energy, throughout American History, it's either been *boom or bust*. So once again, at least in the Rockies, the boom is on, and once again it can be echoed and exclaimed...

There's gold in them thar hills!

Frontier Fools

*"Nature makes only dumb animals. We owe
the fools to society."*

— Honore De Balzac

For generations and throughout our lives
we've heard the warnings, *don't be fooled*! In
spite of that, *there's a fool born every day*, as is
commonly said. It's not that most people are
really such fools, though many certainly are, but
that our minds are simply being manipulated and
controlled psychologically through certain bias
media sources and misinformation to include
advertising and marketing. This goes on, day in,
day out to where people actually become
brainwashed and deceived.

A good example of marketing deception
would be the overarching claim made by all the
auto insurance companies that they can save you
hundreds on your car insurance compared with
the other insurance companies. Some of them
may, perhaps, be somewhat competitively
cheaper than others, but we can most assuredly
know that for the most part, these ads are all just
inaccurately misleading us. When we wade past
all the fine print and fast-talking disclaimers, the

actual playing field is fairly level. On the other hand, one thing we can be sure of, and it makes sense, is that when it comes to things like insurance, brick-and-mortar businesses these days are usually going to be more expensive to run than web-based businesses, which adversely affects the brick-and-mortar businesses' ability to keep up with competition.

There's definitely a need to think critically when receiving information via the media and internet. For instance, while lying in bed early one Sunday morning, I was listening to a talk radio program where they were supposedly interviewing a doctor about dealing with all of the insufferable aches and pains that most people experience as they grow older. All right, fair enough, after all of those years of occupational and recreational abuse to my own body, I could certainly identify with that. So, I continued to listen with some interest, as this physician further explained in very technical terms, all about the onset of these aches and pains, not only why we are experiencing them as we age, but also just what can be done about it.

Well, after about a half hour of what seemed to be a very informative, professional, and logical discussion of this all-too-common, increasing problem among the aging came the hook. After getting my attention and interest up, she (the good doctor) then said something to the effect...*For a limited time, with a thirty-day complimentary risk-free order of my product...blah, blah, blah*. That's when I just rolled my eyes and reached over to turn the radio off.

Perhaps she may have been an actual doctor, who knows? Nonetheless, I have to say, those kinds of wily sales tactics turn me off completely. They lead us to believe that they are some sort of world authority on this big problem that just happens to be inflicting a large portion of the population, just to get our attention and interest. Lately it seems as though many of these types of aggressive sales approaches are aimed at all the aging baby boomers as the primary demographic left with deeper pockets. It's just snake-oil-sales, all aimed at a bunch of old fools who oftentimes fall for it.

Similarly, back in the earlier pioneer days, there were the *frontier fools* who would gather around the elixir salesman's wagon as he spun his webs of deceit and lies. Some people were suckered into actually believing that these wonder elixirs could cure all the things that ailed them. Usually, the product being pushed on them was just a cheap placebo of mineral or vegetable tonic of some sort.

Today, snake-oil-sales, as they were referred to, are still alive and well, as much if not more than they ever were back in the frontier days. Throughout history, only fools have actually fallen for them though. In today's world, you wouldn't think halfway educated, intelligent people would go rushing to the phone to call that '800' number to obtain these alleged wonderful products just because they promise a new you, or a cure for common afflictions.

Many of the people who are taken every day by these unscrupulous gorilla sales tactics may have actually used some of these risk-free concoctions, and due to the placebo effect mentioned, consequently may have actually believed that it worked when it really didn't. It might have likely all been in their head. The original symptoms, if real, may return, and usually, the only thing cured is the promoters' profit margin.

As time goes by in this modern day and age, and if people are actually getting wiser, then we should all reach a point where we quit falling for these gimmicks. In spite of this, intelligent people continue to be fooled and pharmaceuticals seem to be at the forefront of advertising as they were in the days of yesteryear.

The tactics are nothing more than high-pressure sales aimed at taking money away from the masses. Therefore, it becomes an intelligent choice whether we let them continue to take our money or not. As wise consumers with hopefully a keen sense of anti-BS, we should learn to pass up all of the advertising hype.

So, where do we think all the money being taken from the foolish consumers is going? It's mostly going to all the kings of the mountains atop the pyramids of wealth. Americans should become wise shoppers and stop handing all of their hard-earned money over to those whose obsession it is to exploit the masses for their own economic gain. It's called *demand destruction*, and it brings prices down drastically.

As an example of high-priced, high-demand products that people just can't seem to live without today, let's consider *gas and oil*. The oil companies with their all-time record-breaking profits have brought new meaning to the term *highway robbery*. These corporate high jinks may just as well be pulling motorists over on our roadways, putting a gun to their head, and demanding them to hand over their money.

When it comes to demand, it seems as though some Americans have lost their materialistic minds. I was watching *60 Minutes* on television one evening, just before the *Great Recession* hit, when they were reporting on the escalating trend of bigger and better American homes. According to their report, certain well-to-do people were going into various upscale neighborhoods, and tearing down perfectly good three-to-four-bedroom homes just to rebuild a more extravagant, more elaborate house with more bedrooms and bathrooms than they could ever actually need or use. They were doing this simply for the sake of keeping up with the current most prestigious status quo. Ironically, a lady being interviewed, when asked how many bathrooms were in her newly rebuilt giant home, had to stop and think for a bit before she finally answered, saying, *SEVEN*. Absurdly, it was just her and her husband living there. The same foolish and absurd situation is happening on the high seas with prestigious yachts as well.

Speaking of foolish and absurd, in the theme of cabins and condos, I once came across a piece published by CNBC on Americas most expensive cabins. The number one ranking went to a so-called cabin valued at $49,500,000 located with all the ski condos in Park City Utah. This particular place was 20,000 square feet, had 12 bedrooms, 16 baths, and was situated on just over 60 acres.

Another example of foolish excessiveness before the economic downturn came along was the annual bonuses being given at a number of large corporations around the country. During record-breaking highs of the stock market in 2006, while America's meager-paid military soldiers were putting their lives on the line and dying for the held sake of freedom and democracy, the employees of Goldman Sachs, as a classic example, were each being compensated, on average, in excess of six-hundred-thousand-dollar bonuses. Yeah, *bonuses*. Oh, and the top executives there were each being given bonuses of ten to twenty million dollars. Again, that's just in bonuses. I wonder if any of them owned that cabin in Park City. When asked by a major network news anchor about these outlandish levels of compensation, a spokesman representing one of the Wall Street financial institutions just smiled arrogantly and commented something to the effect that – *parents should hope to be so lucky that their children grow up to become investment bankers.*

I have to say that these excessive people are missing the boat on the way to their yachts. Here we have a planet that may be in serious trouble due to global warming and climate change, populated with a majority of people who can't even afford the basic necessities of life, while the affluent people blindly seem only to care about their own personal possessions and their social status among their own wealthy reference groups. There is nothing wrong with *success* until it turns to *excess*.

Sad to say, at one time, America used to be more of a county based on ethical values and principles. It was a country founded on faith in God and decency, with a true reason for pride and patriotism. We truly cared more about the rest of the world, as well as our own less-fortunate neighbors. Obviously, something has drastically changed in this country – *true values*.

America has since become a symbol of greed, mostly resented by the rest of the world. While many people in poorer countries are forced to go without, many Americans have had far more than they could ever need or want, yet they continued to crave needlessly and consume voraciously far more than the rest of the planet. With the Great Recession, that picture was suddenly changing.

Prior to the recession, while America was living the good life on credit, people were being taken advantage of by highly competitive, affluent segments of our society that all but officially took over power and control of this country, as well as the government. The recession should have been a wakeup call.

A major point of this book to make is that while our ancestors may have struggled to make a better life for themselves on the frontier, a life of mostly high values and principles with a sense of decency, community, and civility, many of us as their descendants have since tossed aside those ideals. In that realm, I believe it's time for what's left of the moral majority, who still have some ethics, to stand up together and fight back to reclaim America and make it a country to be proud of again. It's time to stop being controlled and manipulated by greed. In that manner, it has come time for America to wake up, and for enlightened Americans to stop being *fooled* continually into buying things that they truly don't need or require. As we have witnessed happen throughout the free world, in a consumer-based economy, given enough credit by the loan sharks, people can be shrewdly coaxed to consume their way right into the poor house.

When we buy products and services, we need to stop and think about where those dollars are going. That choice should always remain ours, and no one else. It's a simple principle called *supply and demand*. Common business practices dictate that prices will fall when excessive demand goes away. Some time ago, for example, I was standing in Walmart comparing all of the popular brands of over-the-counter stomach acid reducers on the market. The top brands were all selling for more than $20, while the *exact* Walmart equivalency was selling for only $4. No wonder we're all having stomach problems these days. It pays to shop and compare. What do you think would happen to the price of the name brands if everyone suddenly stopped using them and started buying the $4 product?

On all fronts, people need to regulate supply by controlling demand. I can't speak for anyone else, but personally, I'm sick and tired of hearing about how many tens of millions of dollars that the latest movie brought in at the box office, and how much entertainment celebrities make, or how much professional sports teams are paying their athletes and coaches. Furthermore, I'm beyond weary of all the excessive advertising being crammed down our throat every waking moment of our lives. Finally, I'm nauseated from hearing of how much executives are being grossly overpaid in relation to the rest of hardworking Americans these days.

Like the famous anti-drug campaign once coached us...*Just say NO*! Average Americans need to finally put their foot down and say, *enough is enough*! It's time to stop the expensive supply fed by our own excessive manipulated demands. We all need to stop being such fools! Do we really need that snake-oil after all? We should have enough self-discipline to put our money where it really matters, and quit throwing it out the window. Sure, of course, we all need to eat, be clothed, and seek shelter to live even a basic lifestyle, and, granted, we do need to at least entertain ourselves to some degree, as well as recreate and socialize from time to time. However, we don't really need to surround ourselves with a bunch of materialistic crap and expensive entertainment to live a reasonably comfortable and happy lifestyle. Let's spare the landfills from filling up so much and so fast. That said, we should seriously stop using single use plastics since microplastics are invading every corner of the world.

It's true that the best things in life are actually free, or at least fairly cheap. When it comes right down to it, we Americans are quite capable of being creative at entertaining and amusing ourselves when we need to, without spending a lot of money in the process.

Back on the frontier, most people only bought what they absolutely had to, and creatively made the rest of the things they needed or wanted. That level of creativity has since left most of us. However, on the heels of the Great Recession, we were in what was being referred to as the *Great American Reset*. In that regard, it truly was a *reset* in the fullest sense of the word, in that we needed to relearn how to live creatively and sensibly.

I used to be strapped to corporate or government jobs that paid well enough to make everyone else that I was buying products and services from better off than me. Today, I have finally managed to get rid of all the mortgage payments, the car payments, the credit card payments, and all of the associated interest that was going out the window because of them. Today, I live a modest but adequately comfortable lifestyle on around two thousand dollars a month, and live in a smaller, fairly average home that's paid for, drive an average used vehicle that's also paid for, and I never let my credit card balances get to the point where I can't pay them off each month. Furthermore,

I've gotten to where I can pass up trendy, expensive pastimes, and have since found other enjoyable, much less expensive things to do instead. Most residual money left over in my budget goes to savings rather than discretionary spending.

People who have in the past felt that they had to *have it all*, need to reset themselves. Americans need to stop living beyond their means, quit living pretentiously, and learn to live in moderation. Additionally, they need to stop going in debt just for the sake of feeding their own egos and the egos of those around them.

We should stop concerning ourselves so much with what others think. The more we care about what others think, the more we are influenced by them, and the more undisciplined we become while trying to gain their shallow approval. What's *really* important is what we think about *ourselves* and not what others think about us. Why should any of us really care what others think about us if not for the need of acceptance? When a person finally reaches a true state of maturity, they have no need to be accepted by others. At that level of wisdom and enlightenment, they simply know that the people that truly matter to them will always accept them, and will accept them *unconditionally*.

Furthermore, in the interest of our own growth, just as it is better to give than to receive, it should be far more important for us to accept others, with all of their faults and differences, than it is for others to accept us. For people not to accept each other, for whatever sociological reasons, is just plain prejudice. Only people lacking self-esteem, who haven't yet learned to love and respect themselves, will waste their time and money occupied with a longing or craving for acceptance by others. In that regard, if people stress upon themselves to be materialistic, then they're fooling themselves in thinking they need acceptance by others who they may perceive as being important. The only important person that can truly affect and control your life is *you*. Until we learn to love and respect ourselves, we will never be accepted by anyone truly important to us, and people outside of that frankly just aren't worth the bother. Either we have the respect of others, through our own genuine thoughtfulness and trustworthy actions, or we don't. Moreover, if our thoughts and actions are not based on true values and ethical principles, then we probably have a personal problem.

The true decisive test is this: can we sleep at night with a clear conscience knowing that we have done our best to serve humanity without exploiting others, and to protect the world and its environment to the best of our ability? Have we contributed at least something toward making this world a little better than the way we found it? Or have we just blindly been consuming our lives away, immersed in our own selfish interests and programmed desires?

Not to say we won't die tomorrow, but contrary to popular belief, we should quit living our lives in vain as though we *are* going to die tomorrow. In the end, when it's all said and done, if we haven't finally grown up and gotten away from shallow materialism and vanity, then we will have ultimately failed in this life.

If we're determined, however, to be a true success, one that God and our grandmothers would be proud of, then perhaps it's about time for us to get our affairs in order and stop acting like a bunch of *frontier fools*. We should spend our money and our lives wisely in service of others instead of in service of ourselves. That would include serving the planet and all of its creatures as well. What most people fail to realize and understand is that when we focus our lives on others rather than on ourselves, the world (Nature) will reciprocate, and true rewards will *naturally* come back to us.

So, let's not be fooled; ego, which often goes hand in hand with the need for acceptance, is also the need to control. Often, in personal, non-personal, or professional relationships, we can see people with the need to be accepted being manipulated by those who have a need to control. The problem with that entire scenario is this: who of us can really tolerate others attempting to control us, and what given right does any of us have to control anyone else for that matter? Bullying is a prime example of the immature need for power and control over others. Extremes of the appetite for power and control often turn violent. Being a smaller, quiet kid while growing up, I dealt with my share of bullies, but I learned to just smile and be friendly with them first, before they had a chance to be mean and controlling. They never bothered me much after that.

All of that being said, one of the primary goals and missions in life, I truly feel is finally achieving a non-ego state where none of us has either the need for acceptance, or a need to control others. I'm talking about a state where there is at least as much cooperation as there is healthy, ethical competition. To achieve that state may take time, but it will also take a very sophisticated level of training and education, including wise parenting and mentoring throughout the world. To that end, the next generations have their work cut out for them. In the meantime, I can only hope and pray that the rest of us can eventually no longer choose to continue being such fools.

Growth and Change

"It's not the strongest of the species that survives, nor the most intelligent, but the one most responsive to change."

— **Charles Darwin**

I often wonder; are we the only technologically advanced civilization to have ever inhabited Planet Earth? Looking beyond the Adam and Eve theory, I have to belief there could have been other advanced civilizations that lived in ancient times, long before the oldest civilizations that we currently have anthropologic evidence. Furthermore, it's possible that these other civilizations could have evolved to have become more technologically advanced than we humans are today, since we, ourselves, are actually just beginning to become technologically advanced. After all, much earlier European civilizations, which we do have record of, were in many ways more innovative and advanced in such things as architecture and basic engineering than some societies seen in the world today.

This theory also stands to reason because we keep finding the eroded remnants of past civilizations on sea floors and in excavations around the world, which only represent the actual remains of relatively recent civilizations that existed, and which Earth's natural forces have not yet completely recycled. With that, anthropology itself only has a certain window of opportunity to collect any remaining evidence of past civilizations before Nature reclaims and recycles everything from that period of time. With Planet Earth being more than four billion years old, even a diamond will, over enough geologic time, be eroded and dissolved back into free carbon with no clue that the carbon molecules were ever part of the crystalline lattice structure of a diamond. Since Nature recycles and breaks down eventually everything on Earth into its basic molecules and elements, there may simply be no trace whatsoever of any of these ancient civilizations left detectible to us anymore.

Therefore, if there *were* previous advanced civilizations on Earth, something must have happened to them for them not to survive the ultimate test of time. Obviously, without any evidence, no one can possibly know. If they did exist, perhaps they could have been eliminated by natural or unnatural disasters, or, possibly their ability to govern themselves eroded and broke down over time and they wound up destroying each other in acts of world wars using highly advanced weapons of mass destruction.

Lord knows, looking around, we could be headed for the same demise.

Baring disasters and acts of war, I have to wonder what exactly will be our own fate. It has yet to be seen if people in this day and age can come to their senses in time to fully cooperate together for our future wellbeing. As imperfect beings, when will we admit we have, so far, failed at governing ourselves due to our opinionated ways and lack of unconditional love and respect for one another?

I fear that greed and corruption, quite possibly, could send our own civilization down the wrong path toward extinction. I will tell you this: the civilization that finally wises up, figures this out, and commits itself to live with conviction to the ethical standards, which have been so resisted in the past and present, may become the civilization that survives.

The problem with the current state of America, for example, is that those who are in power and control keep handing themselves rewards and benefits from the public coffers via corrupt public and private sectors. Anyone with an ounce of economic sense can see that this self-serving situation simply cannot sustain itself in the long run, and that something significant must happen to turn things around.

Children often do stupid things when they think the grownups aren't watching. Are we so arrogant to believe that we are the only source of intelligence in the entire universe, and that we are not being watched with a critical eye? Even the most intelligent scientists in the world have not yet begun fully to understand what is really going on behind the universal scene. Einstein himself had only started to touch upon it. Perplexingly, what exactly *is* the 'E' that stands for energy in his equation $E=MC^2$. Do we really even know what pure energy is, or where it ultimately comes from? Like ants living in an ant pile, compared with humans living in cities, in relation to the universe as a whole, we humans are probably extremely unintelligent compared with certain civilizations that might exist elsewhere in the universe.

I have previously written about and equate this situation to our pets' inability to understand the technology that we humans now take for granted. In the same respect, it makes sense that we humans, like the ants, remain ignorant of higher universal knowledge beyond our own limited knowledge.

Scientists are beginning to realize that there is far more to everything than we ever suspected. For example, there may actually be more than three dimensions – in fact, there may be as many as eleven dimensions. They are also beginning to discover that there may be multiple universes as well. Suffice it to say, there are things about the universe(s) that we haven't a clue of, just as there are things about our society and our technology that the early frontier people, in their day, would have been dumbfounded by and not have imagined we'd be doing today.

There has to be far more to everything than what meets the eye or crosses our senses. People who believe that they are highly intelligent are to the contrary completely ignorant, since the total combined intelligence of all humans that have ever existed likely represents only a nano-fraction of what there is yet to know. In that respect, we meager mortals essentially know next to nothing, yet many of us continue to think we know practically everything. Fortunately, people are capable of gaining knowledge and wisdom.

In retrospect of my own previous perceptions of the world compared to my current ways of thinking, I can see the change in my life. For example, when I was a young man, I was an avid outdoorsman, hunter, and angler, but as I grew older and became more influenced by Nature and the environment, my overall thinking, as well as my interests, began to change. I now realize that Nature's Law of the Wild commands respect among all animals. One of its primary rules, as part of the natural food chain, is to kill only when hungry. For that reason, I now have a higher respect for all life forms, and no longer have an interest in taking the life of other living creatures unless my own life depends on it. I believe the following quote best describes this higher level of thinking:

"Man is truly ethical only when he obeys the compulsion to help all life which he is able to assist, and shrinks from injuring anything that lives." — Albert Schweitzer

With that, it sickens me to think of people out there illegally poaching wildlife just for the sheer sport of it, especially with animals that happen to be on the endangered species list.

I think the mind shift to serving others has much to do with the education that I obtained while attending graduate school at Regis University in Denver, along with the following Scripture from Matthew: *Verily I say unto you, inasmuch as ye have done unto one of the least of these my brethren, ye have done unto me.* I believe that is partially why I felt compelled to enter the federal prisons to serve as a teacher. After all, prisoners are specifically mentioned within that very set of Scriptures.

In the interest of growth and change, I've been through a number of life's unpredictable cycles, as well as mid-life crises, and I don't know that we ever become immune to them, especially when the esoteric forces and powers in control have more lessons for us to learn. I believe that is ultimately all part of the learning, growth, and change process that is required before we can graduate to the other side of our physical being into the spiritual realm. In that respect, I've learned to pay more attention to the natural signs being presented to me, along with my intuitive feelings. We should listen to the *wind in the willows*, so to speak, and follow our gut feelings to feel and know, naturally, when we are in accord with Nature.

We don't use our minds enough anymore while delegating computers to do much of our thinking for us, such is Artificial Intelligence (AI). Before modern technology took hostage of our brains, humans used to sit down and read libraries full of books. When their eyes grew tired from reading, they would shut them and use their minds to imagine and think, often resulting in creativity, innovation, and invention. Today, this process is called meditation, and it can be a good tool to aid us in that creative effort. Additionally, through meditation, we can grow, change, and gain the ability to achieve the self-discipline and spiritual wisdom needed to control all of our materialistic anchors, urges, temptations, and vices that act to weigh us down and keep us from growing and advancing.

I don't think most people know *how* to meditate anymore because their minds are usually going a thousand miles an hour while multitasking immersed in high technology. Meditation is quickly becoming a lost art.

If we were serious about meditation, we would get out of our vehicles and away from our electronic devices and find a place where we could sit in complete peace and quiet. The middle of a forest, on a quiet beach, or on top of a mountain are places that usually work well for that. We've all heard the phrase *stop and think*. That's all meditation is – stopping and thinking – but we first have to stop before we can begin to think. Cowboys on the wide-open range of the frontier no doubt probably spent a lot of time thinking if not actually meditating.

Thank God I haven't given up my ability to resist the modern ways of the world, and can still meditate. In spite of everything, I can enter a state of mind, without going to sleep, where, like sleep, hours can go by as though they were minutes. During that state, some enlightening and creative thoughts sometimes flow in and out of my head. I've reached the ability now where I can do this practically anyplace, anytime. I don't really need to be in a secluded, quiet place, although I can meditate much more freely in those types of environments. With enough practice, people can meditate anywhere – at some boring social event, while out on a walk, or even while sitting in an airport terminal on layover. Though far from having it perfected, the more I practice it, the better I seem to become. It's a great tool to use when traditional boredom begins to set in, because it often prevents me from just getting in the car and traveling aimlessly somewhere to do something just to entertain myself, or waste money on something I don't really need.

I suppose I have now taken my ability to meditate to the next level as a writer. I just write what I think and feel. My thoughts sometimes subconsciously flow from some source, and at times, while away from the word processor, I will have a premonition that unless I make note of it, will quickly escape me.

Ultimately, I have come to believe that meditation is a process whereby one gains the means to tap into another source of information or energy outside of the physical realm that we live in. It's hard to explain to someone that doesn't have a spiritual sense, or a serious sense of faith, since it's based on exactly that. If you've read much of the material written by Dr. Wayne Dyer, he reflects and communicates this principle rather well.

I truly think that it is highly possible for humans to enter a state of mostly continuous meditation, where we are able to conduct the activities of our lives while, at the same time, in tune with the controlling spiritual forces of the universe – one with God, or one with Nature, so to speak. In this state of mind, our lives and destinies can be indirectly controlled and guided through serendipitous coincidences that present themselves to us day in and day out, as well as in our dreams while we're asleep. This level of insight and enlightenment helps to steer us away from our vices, temptations, and bad habits that would otherwise distract and redirect us down other less-desirable paths in our lives. Provided we pay attention, it's simply our conscience bothering us and tapping us on the shoulder from time to time when we're doing something we shouldn't really be doing. It is a spiritual insight and level of higher consciousness given to us, I believe, by universal forces that we cannot otherwise imagine.

The early Native Americans had knowledge and wisdom of this spiritual source of natural energy, but more contemporary cultures have since diluted that level of insight. Obviously, many people today no longer have a conscience guiding them anymore. Though the potential is always available to everyone, few take advantage of this intuitive ability, and for some, they may never experience it at all unless they learn to open their mind to it.

As I suggested, our own ability to capture and tap into this energy is primarily dependent on our own genuine conviction of true spiritual faith. Either one has true faith or they don't. There *is* no middle agnostic ground. Paradoxically, it is virtually impossible for a person without undivided faith to meditate and tune in to these universal powers and sources of energy, much as it is impossible to tune into a radio or television station without having a radio or a television. That is exactly why those without faith cannot meditate effectively, and consequently become skeptical of the actual ability or the real powers involved with it.

That said, spiritual meditation becomes a paradox. Should anyone happen to remain skeptical of it, then they are frankly at odds of never knowing what it is that they have the power and ability to do.

Meditation and intuition both act to protect and lead us in the right directions. For example, children intuitively may sense danger, but like small animals, predators often overtake them. Case in point, we live in a world where adults in positions of trust are immorally preying upon innocent children of all ages, and where this level of immorality has surfaced even in the clergy. That said, child and adolescent sexual abuse in the world is a growing problem due to the decaying morality of our society.

Like wild animals, for our own safety, we humans should have the intuition to sense danger and disasters unfolding around us in order to take appropriate action to save ourselves. As this chapter suggests, it thus becomes imperative that we *grow and change* for our own good. With danger and disasters, intuitively, like the proverbial *canary in the coal mine*, animals are often barometers of dangerous environments. It is a proven observation that they can naturally sense unsafe conditions, pending disasters, before they actually happen. Again, I believe that the reason for this is that an energy source or collective conscience exists for them to naturally sense and tune in to, but that we humans in our sheltered environments have mostly lost touch with that part of Nature. The term *senseless* in that manner has more literal meaning.

Further speaking of growth and change, when new societies first start out, as did the frontier people in this country, change was not only good, it was essential. The evolution of agriculture not only benefited the mind and body of those who worked the land, but also those who reaped the literal fruits of their labors.

At some point, though, if *uncontrolled*, change has a tendency to backfire. History has proven that civilizations will only improve and prosper as long as the improvements are in the best interest of all its citizens. On the other hand, when those in power and control become corrupt and possessed by greed to the point where they are the only ones that benefit from additional change, then the scales start to tip, and that civilization, as a whole, begins to slowly but surely deteriorate.

When societies weaken, sometimes other stronger outside cultures step in to gain power and control. In the case of America, we are further at risk of having other countries invade us either financially or physically, as the pioneers did with the Native Americans back in frontier times. As for the Native Americans, obviously the changing frontier was not exactly in their best interest. In that situation, immigration can overwhelm native cultures, leading to violence, as it threatens to again in these modern times we live in now. In a competitive world, strength will always predominate over weakness, whereas in a cooperative world, strength will act to help buildup weakness. Historically, people have been far too competitive while lacking cooperation. Consequently, society has regressed instead of progressed.

Additionally, when certain societies display values which become too liberal or too conservative, to an extreme, those civilizations eventually will become unstable as well. Many historians may be familiar with the works of Alexander Tyler, a Scottish history professor at the University of Edinburgh during the time that the thirteen original States of America and the American constitution were being founded. In Tyler's research, he referenced the Athenian Republic some two thousand years prior to the conception of the United States. He insightfully said that, "*A democracy is always temporary in nature; it simply cannot exist as a permanent form of government. A democracy will continue to exist up until the time that voters discover they can vote themselves generous gifts from the public treasury. From that moment on, the majority always votes for the candidates who promise the most benefits from the public treasury, with the result that every democracy will finally collapse due to loose fiscal policy, which is always followed by a dictatorship."*

Tyler indicated that the average age of the world's greatest civilizations from the beginning of history has been about 200 years, give or take, and that during this time, these nations progressed through the following sequence:

> From bondage to spiritual faith.
> From spiritual faith to great courage.
> From courage to liberty.
> From liberty to abundance.
> From abundance to complacency.
> From complacency to apathy.
> From apathy to dependence.
> From dependence back into bondage.

America is likewise on this natural course of destructive regression. Professor Joseph Olson of Hamline University School of Law in St. Paul, Minnesota has indicated that the United States is somewhere between the "complacency to apathy" phase of Professor Tyler's model, with nearly half of the nation's population already having reached the governmental dependency phase.

President John F. Kennedy warned us, *"Ask not what your country can do for you, ask what you can do for your country.*" Sadly, to the detriment of America, this country is increasingly being blindsided by greed and corruption.

So, the question remains; *is growth and change good or bad*? It certainly seems to be inevitable. It was Plato who wrote, "*The only constant is change.*" However, when people resort to *regressive* change while resisting *progressive* change, that change is often followed by crises. The *wildcards* of change, as futurists refer to them, are all too often cultural changing disasters like great depressions and recessions, world wars, pandemics, and natural as well as manmade disasters. America and the world are currently going through so much of this uncontrolled growth and change that it is beginning to be overwhelming.

Closer to home, regardless of the scale and magnitude, we all have a personal need for growth and change as long as the results are positive. However, if we're struggling to make ends meet these days, as many people are, that can tend to interfere with personal growth, sometimes to the point of personal crisis. That's when people tend to lose control of their lives and when others begin to control them, a situation not easily escaped.

Planting the seed of personal prosperity and getting out from under the thumb of power and control of others is possible, but it takes discipline. Financial freedom is a key to true independence, as well as avoiding personal crises, but it takes a certain amount of self-control to stay the course. Unless we have fiscal discipline in our lives, we will continue to spend everything we make, or more, to the point where we find ourselves buried in loans and credit card debt. That's obviously what the predatory loan-sharks that lend all that money at relatively high interest rates want. Unfortunately, many undisciplined people eventually find themselves in such a financial mess that they may have to declare bankruptcy. If they'd only had a little financial knowledge and discipline, they might not have gotten in over their heads so deep.

Back on the macroscopic level, governments and businesses are no exception to the rule. Previous ancient societies as mentioned earlier, including the Roman Empire, probably lacked enough discipline in the end to grow and change enough in the right directions to survive and thrive – leading them to crises as well as the point of nonexistence. America and its people have grown and changed a great deal since the frontier days, but now, in this age, seem to lack the discipline required to get where we need to go for the future. We once were one of the greatest nations in the history of the world, as was the Roman Empire, but something happened to America, as once happened to Rome. Like the Titanic, full steam ahead, not applying the rudders of progressive change in the right directions in time, is not always the best policy.

I can only hope and pray that America and the rest of the modern world can eventually come together to combine their education and technology with discipline to grow and change in the right directions as well as prosper and thrive in peace.

Perhaps the final civilization that pulls it all together, idealistically, through *effective* growth and change, will create the everlasting promise land where there is supreme knowledge and wisdom, unconditional love and respect, perpetual peace, and a true civilization void of suffering and pain as we currently know and experience it.

John Lennon expressed it best in the song *Imagine…I wonder if you can.*

Eclectic Economics

"Economic growth without social progress lets the great majority of people remain in poverty, while a privileged few reap the benefits of rising abundance."

— John F. Kennedy

Money, power, and politics have always been at the heart of world unrest, as well as major barriers to world peace. Therefore, understanding world economics and politics is crucial to understanding and effecting progressive change going forward into the future. Throughout history, there have been those who certainly possessed wisdom in that regard. Here are two of the greatest insights:

"A government big enough to give you everything you want, is strong enough to take everything you have." — Thomas Jefferson

"The inherent vice of capitalism is the unequal sharing of the blessings. The inherent blessing of socialism is the equal sharing of misery." — Winston Churchill

Two basic forces drive the financial markets around the world: *fear* and *greed*. Any market, no matter the economy, can be driven by these fundamental psychological emotions. In the same scheme, what they seem to be teaching indirectly in some of the top business schools around the country is a new form of marketing – *sell with fear*. Remember Y2K? That turned out to be one of the biggest marketing scams of all time.

Seems some people will do anything for money. What is it with money and power that there are people so obsessed with them that they would stoop to such despicable things as robbing elderly people of their hard-earned retirement savings. Consequently, the risk of investing for retirement now has become as much of a gamble as walking into one of the casinos in the historical mining towns of Colorado.

Furthermore, why is it that whenever we hear about white-collar crimes committed on Wall Street, all too often, there are élite business and law school educations involved? What kind of ethics are these schools teaching our future business and government leaders anyway, and what exactly gives their graduates the right to manage large organizations and governments without a substantial amount of qualifying experience under their belt?

I happen to respect those people who've built successful businesses from scratch through their own blood, sweat, and tears, but I have a real problem with the over-educated and under-experienced at the top of our private and public sectors. All too often, the greed and corruption of many of these individuals are what lead societies into economic chaos.

Many people with silver-spooned backgrounds wouldn't know what it's like to have to grow up surrounded by poverty while forced into lackluster careers that involve manual labor. In bad economies, the affluent possess the knowledge, wealth, and power to keep America solvent, but due to their highly competitive nature with each other, they act to hoard wealth, and are usually the first ones to start complaining the loudest about having to pay more taxes. No matter the tax rate, the rich would still be rich. I have to agree with billionaire Warren Buffett, one of the wealthiest men in the world, who implied during the Great Recession, that in an economic downturn, the rich are the only ones left who can afford to bail the economy out when everyone else is broke. After the crash and during the congressional impasse on budget reform, Buffett said, "*My friends and I have been coddled long enough by a billionaire-friendly Congress. It's time for our government to get serious about shared sacrifice.*" It's comforting to know that there are some benevolent wealthy people still left in the world.

It stands to reason that the most successful Americans have a moral obligation if not a duty to pay back a free society that allowed them to become so successful in the first place, especially when that society faces serious austerity measures. It's a simple concept called, *Pay it Forward.*

The Obama Administration, in 2011, proposed that Congress overhaul the tax code and impose what it called the *Buffett Rule.* That rule said, *"People making more than $1 million a year should not pay a smaller share of their income in taxes than middle-class families pay."* Obama was also quoted as saying, *"It is wrong that in the United States of America, a teacher or a nurse or a construction worker who earns $50,000 should pay higher tax rates than somebody pulling in $50 million."* Additionally, one has to wonder about the elderly affluent people in this country who may be collecting Social Security or perhaps taking advantage of Medicare when they don't even remotely depend upon them. What's more, there seems to be little to no social cooperation coming from the ultraconservative class represented by that side of Congress anymore.

Unlike today, back in frontier days, communities more cooperatively banded together to support those among them faced with hardship and disaster.

Looking back at my life, coming from a poor family, I didn't exactly have the opportunity of attending an Ivy League college, and was lucky to be able to go to *any* college for that matter. In retrospect, as a pimple-faced kid who thought I knew practically everything, as most adolescents tend to think, my failing economics class didn't exactly change my attitude. I have since come to realize that, at the time, though I may have been extremely bright for my age, I was realistically less than brilliant.

Perhaps my having a tendency to daydream when bored to tears didn't help much, but if I had been paying more attention during that economics class, I might have wised up and not wasted so much of my life working like a slave for those who were just taking advantage of me for their own personal gain. We only need to look back in history to the frontier days when the mine owners were exploiting miners, eventually causing the formation of the Western Federation of Miners, and though we may not like what unions ultimately became, they did at least act to vindicate workers' rights.

As for economics, terms like *Gross Domestic Product* and *Trade Deficit* may not be the most exciting concepts for a young lad more interested in girls than the state of the economy. Nevertheless, if I had been paying more attention, I would have learned that love doesn't make the world go around, as some may think. If I had been more astute, I might have discovered more important things were in play at the foundation of it all. In recollection, I failed to recognize and realize that everyone at the top of the economic pyramid would be competing with and aggressively going after the assets of everyone else.

Although I could not have seen the entire picture at the time, I would have at least seen some of the basic principles of surviving in this competitively crazy world we live in. Additionally, I would have learned the basic economic principles that America's most successful tend to thrive upon while outsmarting everyone else. In a highly competitive world, one can be beaten up mentally and financially as much, if not more so, as physically.

Those who *were* paying attention in economics classes, likely coached and supported from the sidelines by knowledgeable influences, were probably the ones who went on to have lucrative careers in business and/or politics. Obviously, corporate executives and politicians make a lot of money when compared with the rest of society. They, after all, went on to so called *"success"* while most of the rest of the population found itself merely working and living from paycheck to paycheck.

During the American subprime credit crisis that led to the Great Recession, I had to laugh every time I heard *"the need to attract top talent"* as the explanation for keeping Wall Street executive compensations so incredibly elevated. Ironically, in reflection and disrepute, this so-called executive *"talent"* is exactly what keeps putting our economy in the toilet.

In the case of corporate banking executives, they weren't as talented as they were shrewd. They probably had the right influences, competitive grooming, and perhaps paid a little more attention back in those economic classes. They also used bigger terms for things, such as *collateralized debt obligations* (meaning loans) to make everyone think they were so smart.

I've worked in enough large organizations at the middle management level to know that senior executives are not nearly as *talented* as they lead everyone to think they are. Here's the primary principle that the highest paid executives function upon – *increase revenues* and *decrease expenses*. How genius is that? The primary secret that they use to implement this highly complicated strategic plan is simply a strategy of strict discipline and holding others accountable – better known among the organizational ranks as *fear mongering*. Like the Wizard of Oz hiding behind the curtain, making Dorothy and her friends shiver and shake, fear is by far the biggest control lever used to get people to jump through hoops. Fear of not being *promoted*. Fear of being *demoted*. Fear of being *restructured, downsized, reorganized,* or as it used to be more simply referred to…*laid off* or *fired*. In that manner, the social dynamics and fear factors found in large organizations are *hugely* manipulated since fear of failure has always been a prime emotional motivator.

During the economic downfall of the Great Recession, corporations put a great number of people in the unemployment lines while piling unreasonable amounts of work upon those left working. As the country approached the year 2012, many of the remaining workers became so burned out that they began leaving the corporate world even though the unemployment rate was still very high and jobs were scarce at best. Everyone has his or her breaking point.

The last CEO that I worked for used to say that employees fail for one of two reasons – they are either *unable* to do the job, or *unwilling* to do the job. He may have been right about that, but I would have to add: it's a given that employees can, in fact, fail when *unable* to do the job, due to physical and/or mental inabilities. However, if they are *unwilling* to do the job, they may have not actually failed, but have merely reached a point where they can finally see through all the controlling *corporate crap*. If you've ever been in middle management in a large organization during a budget review with upper management, you know exactly what I'm talking about. These budget meetings are usually nothing more than intimidation power ploys by the executives to control finances, in order to increase the bottom line. Keep in mind that the bottom line is what is funding all the exorbitant executive compensations these days. The reality is that the employees are forced to *do more with less* so that the big-shots can *do less with more.*

Many executives either don't get it, or are so blinded by greed that the employees don't matter anymore. What a lot of managers who continue to run a number of our large organizations fail to realize, is that when you treat people with disrespect and disregard, it will inevitably come back to haunt you. In spite of this, in the short term, I don't think they care much due to all the money they're making.

Many of the top executives in the largest organizations are making millions of dollars a year to demand higher revenues and lower expenses for the sake of the bottom line and their own top line. In fact, the average CEO pay for the S&P 500 was $10.8 million in 2010 while the economy was in the tank. Most Americans hardly make a fraction of that over the course of their entire careers.

While brainwashing the lower ranks of employees, the executives like to use the term *promoting excellence.* Are we all stupid or what? Sorry to say, people are idiots for subjecting themselves to all of this exploitive abuse. We only put up with it because of the need to make our condo payments. Bottom line, we do have a choice. I think the phrase goes – *love it or leave it!*

Well, I don't know about anyone else, but I had finally reached my *corporate crap* saturation point and decided to leave it. *No more! I'd had enough! I was out of there! Take this job and...well, give it to some other chump!* As the executives would say, I suppose I had become *unwilling*.

One small problem in taking that drastic measure is the cost of living and the level of personal debt that often gets in the way of this newfound sense of freedom. After all, I had just taken out two creatively financed mortgages on a quarter-of-a-million-dollar condo in Steamboat Springs. Another common problem that happens is that panic and depression can quickly set in. I dreaded the thought of being homeless and hungry while sitting on the sidewalk holding a tin cup out to other people going by.

Sure, it can be rather exhilarating telling your employer where to go. Unfortunately, that short period of bliss soon wears off, and we find ourselves staring reality in the face while beginning to feel a bit anxious dealing with the tenacious world having its hand out. Wait a minute, where did all these bills come from, and where's the money to pay them all? Obviously, the world is a competitive arena composed of those invoicing and those being invoiced. Nevertheless, I was beyond the point of no return – there was no turning back. The trick to stay out of the poor house would be to have enough wisdom and self-discipline to become debt free. Time to sell the condo.

Frankly, most Americans get in debt up to their eyeballs because they don't have enough self-discipline to abstain from all of life's temptations. They consequently allow others to dictate their lives through peer and social pressures leveraged by mass-marketing and advertising, convincing them that to be happy, they just can't live without certain things. Like a bunch of sheep following each other over a cliff, we are all being brainwashed by gorilla marketing schemes controlled by those who may as well just come out and say, *"stick-em-up"*. Adding to that, many of these marketing professionals are now resorting to subliminal measures in their advertising to dig into our pockets even deeper. Yes, people are being brainwashed and robbed legally against their own ill-minded will.

In a consumer economy based on senseless spending, we only need to look at the Christmas holiday to see wallets being raided by a commercialistic retail world that, through aggressive advertising, attempts to make us feel guilty as sin if we don't spend hundreds of dollars on expensive gifts for everyone we may care about. Another example would be the level of legal loan sharking going on, with all of the ridiculous credit card rates, payday loans, and creative financing instruments available to mortgage our lives away (see *collateralized debt obligations* above). Like the board game Monopoly, think about where all that money really goes. Didn't loan sharking used to be illegal? Nowadays, it's just considered *big business as usual*. It has all become far too predatory for anyone's good.

There *is* hope, however, for all of this financial disparity, but to avoid formidable futures, our society must get away from the grips of power and wealth. As mentioned, large organizations tend to create occupational dependency, which is nothing but a form of legal slavery. People obviously have a want and need to break away from its clutches, but somehow can't quite bring themselves to do it. With enough knowledge, self-discipline, and determination, while acting collectively, we, the less fortunate in this one-sided, unfair world, do have the power to turn the tides on those who are exploiting us.

I've been poor more than once in my life, and though I may never be rich, I'd rather not go back to being *dirt-poor*. From now on, I'm determined to control my own destiny and not allow others to control it for me. In that regard, I believe it's time to revert back to the entrepreneurial values and principles that our pioneer forefathers on the frontier had – they didn't start or finish their days by punching a damn time clock! Therefore, in the spirit of the great western frontier, the time has come to rebuild America and bring more family businesses back home.

I suppose I have always been somewhat of a nonconformist; however, in my last corporate position, I woke up one day and realized that it just wasn't where I wanted to be. There I was sitting behind a desk, ten to twelve hours a day, often six days a week, paying most everything I earned to two Wall Street mortgages held on an expensive resort condo in a virtual sea of condos when I would have sooner been living in a simple cabin away from it all. I no longer had control of my personal life anymore. Once again, I had become a corporate middle management slave on a middle five-figure salary, doing an over-demanding job that there really should have been more than one person doing. I was stuck in a rut helping to raise those revenues and cut those expenses, so that all the executives above me could afford their superior lifestyles.

Sure, as I said, it can be scary to walk away from all of that job security and a steady paycheck, and many people just don't have the stomach for it – for those who do, however, welcome to the world of entrepreneurship.

One of the college classes that I once taught in the federal prisons, as part of a certificate program in business fundamentals, is called *Entrepreneurial Operations*. It was a class aimed at giving the prisoners the knowledge and the ability to startup and make an honest living in their own small business when they get out. The following are some of the principles that were taught:

When it comes to being self-employed, with enough faith, we should follow our gut instincts and passions, as long as it's legal and does not violate the rights of others. Provided we *have* faith, knowledge, determination, and discipline, occupational salvation should come our way. After all, Nature usually guides wild animals in the right directions. We, too, can find the ability to survive just as they do.

What was taught is following our gut instincts and desires with enough faith and determination to where we can hardly fail. The idea is to do what we truly enjoy doing and have a passion for, while serving others, and true rewards will follow. At the very least, we'll hopefully be able to pay the rent and put food on the table. Yes, the trick is actually to make a living out of our passions. That knowledge in itself is true power. As the saying goes, *do what you love*! With enough passion, ambition, patience, self-discipline, and faith, people can move mountains, and hopefully have some fun doing it. It simply comes down to a matter of positive attitude.

I often told the prisoners to remember the famous words of Lou Holtz: "*Ability is what you're capable of doing. Motivation determines what you do. Attitude determines how well you do it.*"

Should we happen to fail as entrepreneurs at first, as many most certainly do, then *try, try again*, keeping in mind that failure is just the opportunity of gaining experience and the ability to pick ourselves up, brush ourselves off, and start over with more knowledge and experience than we had before. In the process of doing that, should we have the intelligence to learn from our mistakes, and the guts to carry on, the third time may just perhaps be a charm.

If we figure out a way to actually make a living doing something we truly love to do, it will probably be one of the easiest and more natural legs of the journey into self-sufficiency. It's not exactly rocket science since we have just spent our entire lives discovering all of the things that we love doing, while already having that list compiled somewhere in the back of our mind. That being the case, we should take the time to sit down and actually put that list down on paper. It shouldn't take very long, and once we have the list compiled, we should start prioritizing it in the order of the things we love and enjoy the most.

Now comes the time to get with family and friends, and start brainstorming exactly how to turn the top priorities into a business that will afford us a living. Some truly great ideas can actually come out of that process.

Once we have determined our avenue for self-employment, we'll need to put together a business plan to reflect it. This business plan, to include financials, will be our yellow-brick-road map to follow in our journey from answering dependently to the man behind the curtain, to entrepreneurial independency away from all the wicked corporate witches. Most importantly, we'll need to stick to our business plans like glue if we want to succeed.

Don't expect profits to start pouring in overnight, but if we're persistently motivated and better than the next person at doing what we already love doing, our odds of succeeding improve drastically. It will be critical to have the stick-to-itiveness and self-discipline to overcome failure and all of the setbacks and challenges that will no doubt be experienced. That after all is the secret of success. It's called passion and enthusiasm, and they're the only antidotes for the disappointment and depression that can take the wind out of the sails of entrepreneurs. The day we lose our passion and enthusiasm is the day we may as well put up the '*going-out-of-business*' sign. As entrepreneurs, our business becomes our life, and our life becomes our business.

If we patiently follow our plans, we should find a form of power entering our life from some unexplainable source, and things should start going our way eventually. Again, that's not to say we won't experience some slow times or a setback or two from time to time. Believe me; I've had my share of them. Life is never perfect. We just have to learn to push our way persistently through the hard times and challenges with that entrepreneurial spirit. Try to remain positive and keep in mind that everything in life is cyclic. Cycles are simply a universal law of dynamics. There will always be ups and downs, troughs and crests. Even the frontier people would have advised us not to get too big for our britches and to save for a rainy day. Like the Boy Scouts, *be prepared*. After serving as a chairman of disaster services for a state chapter of the American Red Cross, along with owning and operating a disaster preparedness business, I can assure you those experiences taught me a great deal about being prepared for life's inevitable disasters. Count on them coming along when you least expect it, but more importantly, don't freak out whenever they do.

With all the accelerating world changes and adjustments that are commonplace in this modern age, people who become unemployed or underemployed should always have a contingency plan. Self-employment, at least part-time to start out, can certainly be part of that. If we're miserably punching a time clock, then why wait for the unexpected? We can sooner learn to swim if we force ourselves off the deep end while learning to keep our heads above water to survive. It's called sink or swim. Sometimes we just need to be pushed off the diving board. All of us were born with the natural ability to swim. It's only when fear and weakness get in the way that drowning becomes a real danger.

So just remember that we all have a natural ability, not only in the water, but in any natural environment as well. Shed the inhibitions and don't let fear and weakness get in the way to drown us in problems. In that manner, plans and budgets can be thought of as water wings – without them, we can tire from swimming and risk drowning. Therefore, as entrepreneurs, plans and budgets become critical supports designed to keep us afloat.

Another important thing to take into account is that everyone out there swimming came from the same sinking ship, and the sharks will all be circling. The best shark repellant is learning to just say *"No thank you"*, and becoming street smart against temptation and slick sales tactics. Be sure to do your homework and always shop around, especially for insurance and professional services.

Oh, and stay away from those excessively expensive condos that carry *collateralized debt obligations*.

Better or Worse

"Accept the place the divine providence has found for you, the society of your contemporaries, the connection of events."

— Ralph Waldo Emerson

The words *for better or for worse*, at one time, back in the days of yesteryear, were once considered sacred words of trust, spoken as solemn wedding vows among newlyweds entering a new life together. Of course, those same vows, by tradition, are still used today ceremoniously, but something seems to have happened to their deep meaning along the way as the calendar advanced through decades of time. In western frontier days, though people were hardly saints, divorce was extremely rare and considered taboo. Today, with the majority of all marriages in America now ending in divorce, *for better or for worse* has since become just a shallow verbal agreement consciously uttered aloud in public, while personal disclaimers are unconsciously whispered under the table with fingers crossed. Fewer and fewer contemporary Americans, including newlyweds, have the required level of unconditional commitment and stick-to-itiveness to carry out consecrated pledges anymore. We have become a society of one-sided personal gratification, having little to no patience, with vows too often resulting in broken promises and leading consequently to broken relationships. Something has happened to the concrete values and principles that truly devoted people once held so sacred.

Other than certain conservatives, sorry to say, too many people have lost their personal ethics and honesty, hence becoming untrustworthy. That being the case, to everyone's tribulation, it has become hard to trust anyone anymore – even marriage partners.

Ironically, I was watching television once when they were reporting that Hugh Hefner was marrying for the third time. He was then at the ripe old age of eighty-four, and was engaged to a twenty-four-year-old woman. Remarkably, the engagement ring cost ninety thousand dollars. I don't believe the wedding ever took place, though I'm sure the whole thing was all merely for publicity and preserving his status as the world's most infamous playboy. As for the girl, in so many of these high-profile celebrity relationships, we can be fairly certain that it was a temporary arrangement of convenience just for attention and money.

Although, historically, marriages were usually permanent, *till death did them part*, most now tend to end in psychological disaster. Today, in addition to prenuptials, we have now gone so far as to create legal marriage contracts that conveniently carry term limits similar to life insurance. So why bother with marriages at all?

My own marriage ended after twelve years when my wife didn't seem to care to remain, for better or for worse, in a typical less-than-perfect relationship. An attempt to reconcile our differences proved fruitless. After a short but unsuccessful stab at marriage counseling, even though I was personally willing and determined to try to work things out, she simply opted out and went her own way. Not long after that, she was arrested and convicted of drug trafficking. Damaged from that, though I've tried to have other relationships, they just never seemed to blossom and go anywhere significant. Consequently, I've never remarried. At this stage of that game, with the music stopped and all the sturdiest chairs taken, I've decided that I'd rather just remain single and free than to involve myself in yet another futile relationship that would probably once again only end in heartache. In that regard, like the desperado that the Eagles once sung about, though I have remained fundamentally free, I suppose that freedom has placed me paradoxically within the solitary confinements of my own personal prison.

Over time, the human right to freedom has slowly backfired throughout America. In general, as time progresses, too many people, when given the full reigns of freedom, seem to have a hard time conservatively pulling back on those reigns to slow down when they start to gallop liberally and dangerously out of control. The outcome is the extremes of a liberal society that believes that it can just freely do whatever it pleases, whenever it pleases, however it pleases, no matter who it may offend or hurt. In the final analysis, common decency and the compassion for others in this social extreme tend to go to the wayside, and the people who resultantly are victimized by it usually suffer needlessly after having their own personal rights violated.

Though people may have had somewhat better ethics in the past, there was still much room for improvement. We only need to look to all of the senseless battles that took place between the Native Americans and the frontier settlers during the great migration into the western territories, to see a breakdown of the essential human relations required for the general peace and prosperity of everyone involved. In the past, there has for the most part been enough land and resources available to support everyone adequately. The problem, therefore, fundamentally lies in the perception of scarce resources (scarcity mentalities), which lead to competition rather than cooperation. In a competitive environment, it happens by and large that the weaker minority will lose to the stronger majority. The Native Americans ultimately found that out.

While teaching human relations inside of the federal prisons, I stressed to the prisoners there; that with freedom comes the responsibility not to infringe upon and violate the rights of others. Accordingly, when we violate the rights of others, we can lose our freedoms. To that end, I'm sure the prisoners are able to identify with that particular concept.

My greatest fear, and as far as I'm concerned, the biggest threat to humanity, is a growing world population that has become unaccountably self-centered, unprincipled, lacking ethics, moral values, and love and respect for one another. This would include an increasing portion of the unenlightened people who remain full of prejudice and hate, and who are the continued source of discrimination and rejection, which can lead to anger and violence, or even the extremes of terrorism. In those situations, I'm afraid that the only thing accomplished is the perpetuation of human ignorance.

In the interest of peace, Martin Luther King stood rock-solidly against violence. In that regard, as silly as it might sound, I really don't care for Halloween as a holiday anymore. The reason being is that its central theme is centered on the macabre – such things as horror, terror, blood and gore, death and violence – hardly something we should be focusing upon and celebrating, especially with highly impressionable children. Furthermore, there is far too much of that stuff on television and in the theaters these days, which is a reason why I don't watch TV or go to the movies much anymore.

In my teachings of human relations to the inmates, I stressed that one of the world's biggest problems, throughout human history, has been the continuation of mistrust, anger, and violence due to our distorted paradigms. Again, as I've stressed, one of the worst of these distortions would be the perceiving of scarce resources, which continues to result in unreasonable levels of competition among people, rather than cooperation. The related lessons we should have learned throughout history should be crystal-clear by now, but competition in our society continues to dominate and dictate, like an animal instinct, unable to transform into cooperation as an alternative sense of knowledge, wisdom, and enlightenment. Due to our primitive instincts and personal desires, our ill-perceived competition with each other lamentably controls our actions. It will only be when people truly learn to love and respect each other, and when they genuinely commit to cooperate, instead of compete, that the world will finally be at peace – a reasonable but highly resisted concept.

For better or worse, the people of this planet can continue breaking promises to each other, getting their hair up on their backs, arguing and fighting with each other, for whatever self-serving reasons they may perceive. Alternatively, a more civilized society should finally come to its senses, open closed minds, and start seriously accepting, communicating, and cooperating with one another. Honestly, is there any other course of action if we want the human race ultimately to succeed and survive? Our only choices therefore become either *civilized, constructive survival*, or *uncivilized, destructive extinction*. I fear there *are* no other options.

Dishearteningly, many people in the world seem to ignore, or don't comprehend what I'm proposing here, let alone seriously go along with and get behind it. It's really too bad that more people can't humble themselves in order to respect others, and to act benevolently to elevate those in need and less fortunate. No, mostly the opposite seems to occur, where egos insist on clawing and fighting to get in front of others who stand in the way of their own shallow-minded success. Realistically, too many people fail to realize that their own true success depends on genuinely serving society rather than selfishly serving themselves. Standing in the way of that are too many false perceptions and distorted viewpoints that are acting to filter out true understanding of effective human relations. Honestly, the world could use a paradigm shift of wisdom.

There are, and have always been, too many extreme viewpoints, that exist among many members of society, with all of their diverse political and religious beliefs. People have to learn to drop their stubborn, opinionated ways, open their minds, and start thinking critically and collectively, while giving as much, if not more than they take. What I'm suggesting, given the nature of politics and religion, is that the extremists need to stop stubbornly digging their heals in, and start seriously meeting others on common ground somewhere in the middle, while focusing on the optimum common good of humanity as a whole. That goes for governments as well. In that regard, the best form of government, I truly believe, would be an equal blend or mix of both capitalism *and* socialism, of course void of all forms of fanaticism and fascism. *Everything in moderation* means just what it says, right down the middle. Inappropriately, regardless of the source of political and religious posturing, personal self-centered outlooks usually play out to the advantage of those who have the most power and wealth over others.

For the *better*, people need to avoid the *worse* by going back to the *golden rule* and quit pulling the wool over each other's eyes by playing games with one another in their own interests. Sacred vows, promises, and contracts need to be once again upheld as they mostly were back in the frontier days of history where a handshake and a verbal commitment were, in principle, as good as gold. Back then, outside of ruthless outlaws, most people had more character, integrity, and allegiance to each other than they do today. These days, without a written contract, when making commitments and promises to each other, many individuals, when no one is looking, routinely put tongue in cheek with the wink of an eye, only to do what they damn well please. In that regardless manner, they turn a blind eye to how their actions may adversely affect others. On a larger scale, it can reach the extremes of predatory capitalism, where innocent people are knowingly exploited through highly unethical business practices, and where these practices are too often legally allowed or conveniently overlooked due to the combined corruption of business and government. When this situation reaches a critical point, the exploited masses begin taking their concerns to the streets in protest. That's where things are today.

Optimistically, we saw, in 2011, the overthrowing of certain governments, such as

Tunisia, Egypt, and Libya, in a relatively short period of time by the combined and collective efforts of the citizens of those countries. With Egypt, a corrupt, authoritarian, monarchy government that had ruled for thirty years was overthrown by hundreds of thousands of young people networking over social media to coordinate political activism efforts that acted finally to bring the corruption of government to its knees. Fortunately, Egypt's military took the side of the people and had enough sense not to intervene and get in the way. With Libya, a long-time dictator was overthrown and eliminated in the same manner with the help of NATO forces. Due to the overwhelming success of these activism efforts, other corrupt governments around the world were being put on notice. Let it be a wakeup call to them. It just shows the power and role of modern communications in facilitating needed change.

I can only hope that with the rise of younger generations into adulthood, we are witnessing the unfolding of a new world order, where the main stream of educated young people finally may be accumulating enough communicative power to overcome corruption in order to take back what is rightfully and inherently theirs. Beginning with the *Occupy Wall Street* movements of 2011, mostly young, enlightened people were focused upon cleaning up greed and corruption throughout the world.

Despite this new world order acting to return power to the people, corrupt governments and businesses still led by older, traditional generations continued to cause problems. In retrospect of the corruption and greed that fed the economic crisis of 2008, which led to the Great Recession, we should reevaluate what went so drastically wrong. Large banks and other mortgage lending institutions became ridiculously leveraged (40 to 1) with debt, allowed by the lobbied relaxing of bank regulations on subprime mortgages, and driven by capitalistic competition. With these debt levels on such high-risk mortgages unsustainable, investors started to bet against the mortgage equity packages that were created from them with investment instruments called *Credit Default Swaps*, effectually causing market depreciation and turmoil. Things went sour so fast that the government had to step in to intervene and bail the crisis out. Under the circumstances, the government implemented complicated, burdensome rescue plans, all paid for by the taxpayers. Those who were originally in power and control of the situation, including Congress, were acting in narrow, short-term interest, and not in the broad, long-term interest of the public. Consequently, *it all went south*, would be a famous expression that would apply to what happened after that. It became hard to distinguish the cops from the robbers – or shall we say the sheriffs from the outlaws. Either way, the *lawmakers* were conspiring with the *lawbreakers*, and no one, but no one, was being indicted throughout the whole process. Justice not being served proved how corrupt big business and government had become.

As all of this was unfolding, I left South Fork to oversee risk management for Steamboat Resort in Steamboat Springs. There, as previously mentioned, I purchased the small one-bedroom condo near the ski resort, but reluctantly had to take out two separate mortgages on it. One mortgage was for eighty percent of the purchase price, while the other was essentially an equity loan on the first, designed and disguised to cover the twenty percent down payment required to avoid the PMI (private mortgage insurance). In other words, the lender pulled some questionable strings – *creative financing*. Once all the closing papers were signed, the vast majority of my employment earnings, after that, went to pay those two mortgages. Fortunately, my intuition kept tapping me on the shoulder and telling me that something wasn't on the up and up, and that the housing bubble in America was becoming a bit overinflated. Therefore, after contemplating all of this, I made a sudden and bold move before it actually burst. That's when I sold the condo and went back to South Fork where I still had a log home that was paid for, free and clear – the property that I converted into the B&B. As previously mentioned, my less-than-desirable employment situation at the time also pushed me in that direction.

After going from cabin to condo, as it turned out, I made the right move going back to the cabin. Looking back, that was probably one of the smartest things I may have ever done, since the housing bubble did, in fact, burst shortly after that. It just goes to prove; we should always trust our natural instincts. If I had lost my job, as many did during the ensuing economic downturn, I would have been put in a position where I may have had to walk away from that condo. After that, I could have been forced to sell my other home to cover the damages, and gone back to renting. Worse yet, I could have ended up unemployed and homeless, as many in this country dejectedly came to experience in those days.

Unfortunately, during all of this, I failed to listen further to my intuitive gut feelings, and made the mistake of leaving the bulk of my retirement funds invested on Wall Street. When the bubble finally burst and the market plunged because of it, by the time I caught that falling knife, I (along with many other Americans) had already lost much of my retirement investments. Had I only listened to that voice in the back of my head again, and gotten out beforehand, I could have avoided much of that grief as well.

I suppose in hindsight, we shouldn't blame the government completely for relaxing regulations, making housing more affordable to the lower classes while at the same time accommodating the financial and real estate industries.

We also can't completely blame the subprime homebuyers for wanting to realize the American dream. They were just going along with the lenders and believing them when they were told: *Sure, you can afford the payments, and with the way real estate values are going up, you'll probably be able to sell the place at a profit. Either that, or you can just refinance before the adjustable rates kick in.*

More obviously, the root cause of the problem was the overall pressure on the financial institutions to maintain phenomenal, unsustainable growth by taking on too much debt. To that end, is why the financial institutions had lobbied and gotten bent the laws of regulation in their favor to be able to do that. Otherwise, I'm sure that the lending standards would have remained much stricter in America.

Historically, back in the frontier days, if one needed shelter, they went out into the forest, cut down the trees for a cabin, and built it themselves from scratch. As time advanced, if someone wanted to buy an existing home, unless they were wearing a mask and pointing a six-shooter, the bankers wouldn't begin to give them a dime until they could prove they were actually trustworthy enough to pay the loan back, with interest. Back then, people were also required to put up a certain amount of what was referred to as *collateral* (skin in the game) to secure the loan. In fact, that's the way it always was, right up to the ensuing days of contemporary creative financing. That is, until the high-flouting, publicly traded corporate banks and mortgage houses, with their funny money and financing shenanigans came along, all lobbied among and allowed by Washington.

Related to all of this is one of the many profound quotes made by Thomas Jefferson: "*I sincerely believe that banking establishments are more dangerous than standing armies.*"

With the mortgage lenders being pushed by extreme socialism from one side, and pulled by extreme capitalism on the other, as I previously said, *it all went south*.

In a broader political context, by its own nature, capitalism has always condemned socialism, since socialism acts to interfere with the prosperity of the affluent, which is being supported by the sheer system of capitalism itself. That being said, I find it highly ironic that during these economic downturns, usually caused by competitive greed, governments have to step in to rescue conservative capitalism with liberal socialism. That's why you'll always find me independently sitting the political fence. It should be obvious by now, that's really where everyone else in the world should be sitting as well. I personally go back and forth between conservatism and progression, depending on the issues at hand. Certain things need steadfastly to remain conservative, such as ethics, values and principles, while other things obviously need to change to be more progressive, like the right to quality, affordable housing and healthcare.

Ultimately, the extreme conservatives need to learn to *give* as much as they *take*, while working together with the progressives in the common interest of the majority of the population. Additionally, the extreme liberals must learn to respect the strict, ethical, and traditional values of conservatives. We would all be better off as moderates.

Apart from politics, when you really think about it, the same middle of the road, moderate principles go for religion too. If we took all religions, put them in a blender, and mixed them up into one homogenous blend of religion, we would have a unified form of spiritualism that all could mostly identify with and hopefully respect, if not live by. What if all supreme religious beings throughout history, such as Christ, Buddha, Allah, and Krishna were all basically the same messengers in principle? In my mind, I believe a universal force (*The Force*) is the same one recognized in the movie Star Wars, or *The Force of Nature* in the series Star

Trek, and is, in reality, *God* – the force and source of everything. Though we may pray for elusive peace, we should have faith that it will be delivered ultimately to those of us who fully embrace it.

To reiterate a key concept of this book, in the end, the only way the world will find true peace, is if everyone, together, learns to give and take unselfishly, while recognizing, respecting, and accepting each other *unconditionally*.

With many people, all this talk may seem platitude and idealistic, but I've always been taught that if you can visualize it, it can happen. I certainly don't have a hard time visualizing a truly peaceful world. I doubt that anyone else with any sense of common decency does either.

We would all be better served visualizing and acting upon that world where idealism becomes a self-fulfilling prophecy and reality. Otherwise, with the status quo as it is, people only stand to continue selfishly arguing and fighting among each other, like spoiled children, over perceived scarce resources.

For better rather than *worse*, God willing, at some point, the world could stand to grow up.

Richer or Poorer

"That man is richest whose pleasures are the cheapest…Give me the poverty that enjoys true wealth."

— **Henry David Thoreau**

There once was a time on the western frontier when neighbors who lived miles apart depended upon one another. Without the support of each other, people back then were often highly at risk of danger.

We now live in a time where many people don't even know their next-door neighbors, let alone care much for them. In the same regard, many upper-class people are indifferent to the welfare of the lower classes. Self-centeredness has separated the country to where laws are no longer being made in the interest of the general population, but are lobbied and changed primarily in favor of the rich and powerful. The affluent, as a result, indirectly influence and control government to their own advantage. To that end, as we have seen, the rich continue to get richer, and the poor continue to get poorer. The poor slowly but surely having the hope for prosperity taken away from them, forced into *dependency* rather than *independence* as was originally set forth by our forefathers.

One of America's primary forefathers, Thomas Jefferson, worried that the courts would overstep their authority, and instead of interpreting the law, would begin making law, resulting in oligarchy, or the rule of few over many. The very words he helped to compose, *we the people*, have since become a misrepresentation. Additionally, we must not forget the forewarning words of Alexander Tyler, as previously mentioned, who cautioned that every democracy would finally collapse due to loose fiscal policy. We, therefore, should sit up and take notice; America is no longer a country *of the people, by the people, and for the people*, it has since become a country *of the rich and powerful, by the rich and powerful, and for the rich and powerful.* We now live in a world where a small percentage of the population possesses most of the wealth. In fact, the richest 1% of Americans possess more net worth than the remaining 99%. If allowed to continue, it is yet to be determined among that 1%, who will rise eventually out of the oligarchy to dictate.

All of this is taking place in a world where 80% of the population lives in poverty, 70% are illiterate, and 50% suffer from hunger and malnutrition. Unfortunately, the world remains anything but a civilized place.

Not being so fortunate to be one of the rich and powerful, coming from a poor family, I've had to spend a good deal of my life struggling to make ends meet, while living from paycheck to paycheck, doing less-than-desirable jobs. I seriously doubt, during the Great Recession, that many of the wealthiest went without, or could even relate to the concept of working from paycheck to paycheck, let alone being unemployed with *no* paycheck as many were at that time.

Similarly, there is a huge disconnect between Wall Street and Main Street these days. The investment world has been taken over by institutional traders with powerful computer systems, where large hedge funds with highly sophisticated management teams have become the financial equivalent of gated communities. These lucrative capital investment clubs, afforded only by the wealthy, often requiring a minimum of a million dollars to join, are not feasibly available to the average investor, and like gated communities, most commoners are simply not allowed. Thus, the rich prosper, and successful hedge fund managers are highly rewarded in the process. Michael Thomas, a former Lehman Brothers partner, commented on the lavish behavior going on behind these hedge funds. He said, *"This behavior suggests they are isolated from the rest of the world, living behind these great big hedges."* If you ask me, it all smacks of organized crime. Like organized crime, the ridiculous profits created by these firms are plucked ultimately from the pockets of common people since everyone knows that money doesn't just grow on trees. From where do you think the top 1% gather their wealth?

How can a free society, based supposedly on principle, ever justify conditions where Wall Street investment firms rake in billions of dollars in compensation and bonuses, when millions of innocent children all over the world are literally starving to death? According to James Morris, prior director of the United Nations World Food Program, there are four hundred million hungry children around the world. The U.N. reports that a child dies from the complications of malnutrition every five seconds. That's approximately eighteen thousand innocent children per day needlessly dying of starvation. It will only be by applying enough resources equitably toward education and technology that we will ever be able to head off this appalling condition. As it is, I fear the poor may continue to suffer even more so in the future.

Considering so many go hungry, I once made it a point each year during the Thanksgiving and Christmas holidays to work as a volunteer for Loaves and Fishes Ministries, putting together bags of food and delivering them to the poor and underprivileged. It truly gives one a sense of how fortunate we are to have what many do not.

While delivering food to the impoverished one Christmas, I came to the last address on my list. As I pulled up and parked, I saw a man standing among some tables in his front yard, with both an American and a United States Marine Corp flag proudly displayed. As it was, this poor man, an apparent Marine veteran, was having a yard sale on that cold, gray December morning, trying to raise enough money to have some dental work done. I have to say it was an honor to hand him those bags of food and wish him a Merry Christmas. I'm sure he felt my deep respect rather than my pity. With that, he was humbly grateful and reached out thankfully to shake my hand more than once.

On another occasion, while coming home after volunteering that day, I stopped to get gas and noticed a ragged, elderly man with a disability cane, wearing an old tattered cowboy hat. I could only assume he was homeless, and I thought of all the homeless, disabled veterans everywhere. It was once again a bitter cold winter day that day, as that weathered old man slowly made his way across the street to a drive-up bank where he unpretentiously sat down on a curb to warm himself in the afternoon sun. After I had finished getting gas, I drove over to where he was sitting, lowered my window, and asked him, *"Hey, is this a drive-up bank?"* He just gave me a blank stare and said he didn't know. So, I pointed the bank's sign out to him while handing him five bucks (enough maybe to buy a hamburger or something, but not enough to buy booze). I then told him that I would like to make a deposit, and wished him a Merry Christmas. He just smiled while putting the money in his pocket. As I drove off, some people parked in a truck, directly facing me, gave me their thumbs up, which made the joy of giving that Christmas even more special. At the time, I was only living on a little more than a thousand dollars a month myself, but I figured the old guy needed the money more than I did.

America claims to truly value its military veterans, but I have to wonder to what degree. Here are a few statistics on American veterans: The unemployment rate for war veterans is more than double the national average. Veterans are three times more likely to commit suicide than the general population. Veterans are estimated to represent 25 percent of all of the homeless in the United States. There are no golden parachutes for these guys. Realistically, America values corporate executives far more than it values its war heroes.

Back in the pioneer days, I can imagine that being homeless on the frontier, though tough as it was, might not have been as difficult as it is today. Back then, it was possible to at least build a small cabin or shed and perhaps live off the land. Obviously, the old homeless cowboy that I handed that five to didn't have any housing, and I'm not sure that some of the rundown dilapidated shacks and trailers that I've delivered food to could be classified as adequate housing either.

I can't understand people who have never experienced poverty, and who look down their noses upon the poor and underprivileged while making snide remarks, such as; *those lazy welfare cases could get out of poverty if they would just apply themselves.* Equally callous would be the arrogant viewpoint of big business people concerning the creation of jobs, who say, *I never saw a poor person ever hire anyone.* To that, I would say, *I never saw a poor person ever lay anyone off* or *foreclose on anyone's home.* The number of people who lost their jobs and their homes during the economic downfall of the Great Recession is beyond shameful. Along the same lines, it made absolutely no sense to be laying teachers off while overloading the number of students per classroom when America was falling behind the rest of the world academically. I'm sure the privileged private schools didn't have nearly the economic challenges of the less-privileged public schools. Not only do the rich continue to get richer, and the poor continue to get poorer, but also the dumb continue to get dumber – a primary reason why America is no longer #1 in education.

If certain privileged people weren't so egocentric, then the underprivileged might have more opportunity and half a chance at *applying themselves* in life. The real war in this world isn't the one against the terrorists and foreign enemies. No, the real war going on is class warfare – the *haves* against the *have-nots*. What chance do the poor have against power and wealth? Forget complex macroeconomics and microeconomics, in the final analysis, those having macro wealth and power will continue to insist on micromanaging everyone else.

Throughout its history, especially recent history, America has been in the midst of a perpetual power struggle going on between the classes – the conservative wealth of the few against the dearth of many. Doggedly, this power struggle among the classes continues today, as displayed by all of the bipartisan bickering that goes on, back and forth, in the halls of Congress. We only need to look to the primary sources of political campaign funding to see the manipulative controls being levered behind the scene.

Be it past or present, the power of wealth has mostly dictated, and the unfairness and inequities that come from it have persisted. I'm taken aback by the laissez-faire attitudes among many people that believe that there is really nothing any of us can do about it. To that, I would strongly argue that there are, in fact, things each of us can do, such as the Occupy Wall Street movement for example. I personally can't just sit back and watch greed and corruption destroy this country. I can at least write about it in an effort to raise awareness, and perhaps affect some type of positive change. Otherwise, the appetite of wealth in opposition to the hunger of poverty will continue to feed upon and strip this nation to the bone.

The pathetic story of poverty plays out every day in this country. Another good example would be Camden, New Jersey, considered the poorest, most violent city in America. In Camden, there are drug dealers on practically every corner, and the homicide rate is one of the worst in the world. There, many at-risk children are being raised by alcoholic, drug addicted parents, who have essentially lost control of their lives, unable to guide and manage themselves, let alone their children who are being recruited relentlessly by gangs and drug pushers. Most of these children start out primarily as happy kids with the potential to grow up to be responsible, productive citizens with normal lives and careers, but the environment around them soon engulfs them like wildfire. Relatively few escape the clutches of that terrible world, and far too many end up either in prison or worse – dead.

Appallingly, the money involved in drug trafficking between Mexico and the United States would pay for quality education and healthcare for every man, woman, and child in both countries. Meanwhile, the drug trafficking and the poverty and violence it fuels persist relentlessly due to the money and power involved.

Outside of the unfortunate disparity of poverty, there are those who have relatively so much that they are no longer appreciative. For example, I was watching the *Today Show* one morning during the Christmas holiday when they were featuring a high-hit U-tube video of a young boy opening a Christmas gift to find only books, and having a conniption fit of disgust. The Today Show had both the boy and his mother there in the studio that morning, with the mother arguing that her son was a good boy and was not really spoiled. However, at the end of the segment, the host of the show handed the boy a wrapped gift, assuring him it was not books. The boy quickly tore open the gift to find an expensive talking cowboy doll, exclaiming disappointingly that he already had one of those. In today's less-than-privileged parts of the world, most kids would be thrilled to receive a talking doll. Call me scrooge, but I personally no longer participate in the American holiday gift exchanging ritual anymore. Frankly, I would rather give my time and money to charity instead.

With the underprivileged, carefree and joyful childhoods rarely last, and *happily-ever-*

after is usually nothing more than a fiction fairytale. Even with the middleclass, carefree and happy can have a tendency of turning into unhappy dependency, stuck in meaningless jobs that merely pay the bills, living from paycheck to paycheck, with comparatively little to no residual income or savings to show for all of their hard work. Additionally, as we have witnessed during economic downfalls, many are oftentimes in debt up to their eyeballs in mortgage payments, car payments, and credit card balances to the point of bankruptcy. Involuntary unemployment is often the final straw. Stuck in this rut, their lives can become shattered with hopeless vices and addictions to escape reality. Pick your poison. In that regard people can become slaves even more so to power and wealth, since many a fortune has been made selling addictive vices, such as tobacco, alcohol, and drugs.

Further digging at the roots of the problem; with unhampered freedom and wealth, there comes a point where certain people can have *too* much to appreciate, with many of them grabbing everything insatiably they can get their hands on, even though they may be taking it away from those less fortunate. In the world of children, it's considered bullying, not playing nice, and not sharing. In the grownup capitalistic business world, there are such things as hostile takeovers as they're called. Therefore, bullying and hoarding takes place at all age and status levels. Remember playing musical chairs while growing up? I really hated that game. It taught competitive greed rather than cooperative sharing.

Greed and the lust for power undeniably contribute to conflict. After observing and studying these social dysfunctions for decades, I think I finally see the true human relations of it all. Human beings, especially Americans, are mostly considered untrustworthy because we are raised, or should I say are *brainwashed*, to be highly competitive rather than cooperative with one another, and that's exactly why people come to not trust each other. Mistrust is what destroys relationships. Incongruously, it can be said: *In God we trust, but in man we compete.*

In my first book, *Wise Choices*, the primary premise of that book was based on human society, as a whole, reaching a critical level of knowledge and wisdom required to extinguish its primitive tendencies, such as prejudice, greed, anger, and the resulting violence that can come from it all. Obviously, our world society is nowhere currently near the level of knowledge and wisdom required. Of course, we're gaining intelligence in math, science, and technology to a certain degree, however, we're falling far short and failing futilely when it comes to the level of true intelligence and wisdom required to realize a mutual sense of peace and prosperity.

World powers, public or private, continue to hoard world resources. Looking around, the widening gap or margin between the free world and the third world continues to expand to where there soon may not be left any middle ground. That's a frightening thought that ought to be scaring the hell out of anyone on the wrong side of the tracks who is not fortunate enough to be self-sufficient and independent financially.

Let's not fool ourselves; there's really only one solution to all of this, and that is to take the excessive profits and compensations out of the predatory capitalistic system before it breaks the world's fiscal back. The wealthy continue to prosper financially, which only acts to create further hardship among everyone else. The excessive affluence of some simply does not bode well for the world's overall long-term economic health.

Unfortunately, many less than privileged people in America are headed towards financial destruction and poverty. So, what can be done about it specifically? Well, forget all the king's horses and all the king's men, if we're ever going to put Humpty Dumpty back together again, there's an old well-known phrase that goes, *fight fire with fire*. Now I'm not talking about becoming a radical extremist or revolutionary activist while resorting to violence or terrorism.

Violence has never, and will never solve anything in the world. What I'm talking about is using the power of *choice* to control our own destiny, as well as the destiny and wellbeing of our immediate families and future generations.

The lower classes, to include the weakening middle class, need to wise up and rise up to resist the establishment by not allowing them to turn us over and shake the change out of our pockets while robbing us blind. Simply stated, *if you don't need it, don't buy it.* However, it takes discipline to do that. When hard pressed, families, neighbors, and communities need to stick together with discipline and cooperation as they did back in the frontier days.

Though there are still some solid families left in America, a big problem today is that in many cases the institution of the family has deteriorated to a critical level. Just look at where America came from, and where it is now. Cabins to condos, has America improved compared with its history? It obviously has improved technologically, but not so much otherwise. The foundation that America was founded upon is quickly crumbling away, possibly putting this country at risk of collapse.

Over time, the strength of the American family culture has deteriorated. In many instances, there is no immediate family structure left anymore – meaning a tight-knit group of individuals that truly love and respect each other and who support each other on a daily basis, day in and day out, day after day. I'm referring to people who we wake up to, people that we sit down and have breakfast and dinner with, people that we actually spend quality time with, and people that we miss truly whenever we are separated.

Historically, as a matter of tradition, family ties dominated people's lives, such as in family ran small businesses. Today, those ties are being strained to their breaking point. For us to only visit our *families*, perhaps once or twice a year on over-crowded, commercialized holidays has become a travesty. To our exasperation, the people on the other end are no longer family in the true sense anymore – they're just people that we happen to be related to – *relatives*. Worst yet, with all of the dysfunctional power struggles that go on within families these days, many relatives don't even care to be around each other all that much anymore and are often taxed spending what used to be quality time together. So, what's the point of going to all the trouble of getting together in reunion once or twice a year anyway? Because we know, at least in our hearts, should that ever end; we stand to lose much of the true purpose and meaning in life.

At the heart of it all, the world of big business, for a long time, has been tearing

American families apart. Though the highly demanding, fast-paced corporate world has made so many dependent on them for a living, it doesn't have to remain that way. Again, fighting fire with fire, it's our God-given choice to get off of that merry-go-round if we're really serious about turning things around. There exists a better way of life to go back to, but we have to redefine our value systems in order to achieve it. Thus, we have what's been referred to as the *Great American Reset*. The philosophy and culture of doing whatever we want, whenever we want, wherever we want, and buying whatever we want whenever we want it, just because we've been brainwashed mostly through media marketing to do that, is living a lie. Provided we have a close-knit family, we only need what we need when we need it, and despite what all the commercials keep telling us, self-centered egos, materialism, and vanity are not required to be happy.

Spiritual faith and family are undeniably a prerequisite to, and a requirement of success, no matter what one's ultimate goals happen to be. Without them, the structure of our lives is at risk of being destroyed by disasters, be they natural, domestic, medical, financial, or otherwise. If you didn't before believe that, hopefully I have opened your eyes so that you can at least now better see and understand that. If you happen to agree, and support what I'm saying here, then you're likely already well on your way to true success and happiness, if not already there.

Looking back at my own life, it has become quite apparent to me that I was most successful whenever I put my friends, family, and community first and foremost. The foundations of my life started undeniably to crumble and fall apart whenever I lost focus of the importance of the critical infrastructure of people around me that not only supported me, but also loved and respected me, *unconditionally*, on a daily basis, no matter what obstacles I faced. That principle of life is like night and day – either we see and experience the enlightenment of it, or we're left in the dark with only the anguish of our own lonely egos.

The principled foundations of our lives, therefore, are the cornerstones of happiness, and the structures of those lives can only be as sound as the attention given to their design and construction. The architectures of our personalities and beliefs are therefore critical to becoming strong people, resistant to all of the harsh elements that we can't help but to be exposed to throughout our lives. Psychologically, there is no such thing as having a *sheltered life*. Everyone, no matter what walk of life they may come from, rich or poor, is at risk of mind eroding elements.

If we just stop and think back to our childhood, we will remember either a spiritual faith-based supporting environment, or not. Those who grew up in that type of environment already have a distinctive advantage over those who didn't. That's not to say that those who grew up in an underprivileged, abusive, or broken home environment, which may have been void of true faith, can't achieve success and happiness. On the contrary, they certainly can, but they may have a few more obstacles and challenges to overcome.

Even people without the tools of faith and family are capable of backing up to obtain them. They just need to have the desire and sheer determination. Oftentimes it takes a major crisis or even a surmountable series of crises to come into our lives before we begin to understand those messages being presented to us, and before we can actually change. Self-centeredness and loneliness are most certainly life crises, and with a weak and crumbling foundation in the structure of our lives, crisis not only causes change, it can cause *disaster*.

For richer or poorer, before we ever stand a chance of building a better life and becoming successful and happy, it is most imperative that we get our foundations in order. Ethical values and principles along with the genuine concern for others will always need to come first and foremost in our upbringing. Prosperity, and paying it forward from that, can only be built upon that foundation. Nothing else in our lives will ever matter otherwise.

Sickness or Health

"The groundwork of all happiness is health."
— **Leigh Hunt**

Despite today's challenges in healthcare, back in the days on the western frontier territory, there were as many if not more health and welfare challenges as there are today. Fortunately, for the contemporary world, there have been many phenomenal breakthroughs in medical science and technology in recent times than occurred back in the pioneer days. Medical research and development have unquestionably advanced immensely since the days of the horse and buggy when people were lucky if there was a doctor within a day's ride, let alone a hospital available. Back then, people less at risk lived in the more populated eastern cities, close to what was considered the best medical care for the times, but if they became inflicted with illnesses or injuries, those inflictions could have still been quite threatening. Increasing the risk factors, if they had moved away from one of these populated areas and migrated out west, as many did, illnesses and injuries were not only life threatening, they were often downright fatal. One needs only to walk through some of the old cemeteries found in the historic mining towns of

Colorado, reading the tombstones there, to see the frequency and severity of death at an early age, especially among small children.

Today, considering the health risks involved with all of the vices people have, such as overeating, drinking, smoking, and doing drugs, the biggest threat of dying, by far, is from cardiovascular disease, with it having more than twice the fatality rate of cancer. In fact, around seventeen million people a year in the world die currently from heart disease.

My own mother died from heart problems when I was sixteen. She had been left with a damaged heart as a young girl after being inflicted with rheumatic fever, and as a result of that, she later underwent open-heart surgery more than once before she finally died in her early fifties. That's back when open-heart surgery was much riskier and much more invasive than it is today. Today, with modern surgery techniques, heart operations involve far less risk and are often now performed practically through outpatient services. In spite of that, even with high technology saving many more lives today, cardiovascular disease remains the number one killer.

This disease not only took my mother, but my best friend from childhood also died of a heart attack while dirt bike racing – he, too, was only in his early fifties. With heart disease being so prevalent, I imagine most people either have known or know of someone afflicted with it.

Back when pioneers were settling the western frontier, including the Colorado territory, if a person unfortunately suffered a massive heart attack, it was likely the end of the road for them. There *were* no phones to dial 911, and no ambulances or flight-for-life helicopters with EMTs to administer lifesaving procedures. Due to the difficult western frontier lifestyles and the relative lack of medical personnel and facilities, the average life expectancy age back then was much less then than it is today. Then, most people only lived into their forties. Some frontier outlaws, due to the inherent risks of being an outlaw, lived even shorter lives. Two of the most famous were Jesse James, known to have spent time in Colorado mining towns like Creede, who died at the age of thirty-four. Then there was Billy the Kid, who only lived to the ripe old age of twenty-one. Both outlaws' lives ended early due to unfriendly gunfire.

Today, an average healthy person lives well into their seventies, eighties, and nineties, and with the accelerating advances in medical science, it won't be long before people, on average, may be living past the age of one hundred – that is, if they can afford the ever-increasing costs of healthcare and hospitals, not to mention the high expense of nursing homes.

As for hospitals, once referred to as *almshouses*, they were historically ran primarily as smaller non-profit entities by religious organizations, such as the Catholic Church, but have since been taken over by either larger corporations or technically legal non-profit organizations with numerous well-paid executives and professionals. Consequently, the cost of healthcare in America has since skyrocketed, and affordability has all but taken its last breath and flat-lined. Adding to the problem, with increasing age levels, the more expensive supply and higher demand for healthcare services in the future will certainly continue to be a financial challenge, more than most of the aging population will be able to bear.

Back on the frontier, life was much different in many ways than it is today. I often daydream and romanticize about what it would have been like living back in the Wild West days, provided one was healthy enough to survive it. To have pulled up roots on the eastern seaboard and endured the long dusty, sometimes muddy trip west, well, that had to have taken a great deal of physical stamina and a lot of intestinal fortitude. Westward ho, as they said, there were most certainly some incredible challenges to endure, but then again, there were probably also some incredible experiences, as well as all the beautiful, pristine scenery along the way.

Some of the earlier settlers opportunistically came west in droves as a part of the California Gold Rush of 1848, as well as the start of the Colorado Gold Rush ten years later in 1858. Some just came for the sheer excitement and challenge of it. Regardless of what brought them west, many people scattered throughout the western territory back in that era to somehow make a new life for themselves. Historically, some people made their life from mining and other occupations such as merchandising or railroading, but many more stuck to the basics of farming and ranching. I believe if it had been me, at first sight of the Rocky Mountains, I would have also fallen for the romance of the region and thrown the anchor out right here in Colorado. Like some of our ancestors, I, too, probably would have been swayed by the romance of gold and may have filed a mining claim or two as well. On the other hand, more levelheaded and risk adverse, I might have decided to homestead a spread of land where I could have grown crops and raised livestock. In any case, I would have built a sturdy cabin, and if I'd committed myself to farming and ranching, a good barn to withstand the fiercest of Colorado winters. Either way, I would have prayed to God each day to protect my family from harm, and to keep us strong and healthy. It's hard to imagine how difficult it must have been to be struck down with injury or illness and been bedridden under life's harsh environments and circumstances back in that day and age.

When it comes right down to it, though I think I would have enjoyed life back on the frontier, I get to thinking about all the simple things we now take for granted, like hot showers, major appliances, automobiles, or the many other modern conveniences we currently enjoy, and I have to gratefully appreciate the present times we live in.

Whether we happen to be talking about the era of historic frontier cabins or that of contemporary condos, there has always been, and will always be a need to remain healthy, to not only sustain and survive, but to grow and thrive. Without one's health, *physical* as well as *mental*, then what's the point to life anyway? As they say, *when you have your health, you have just about everything.* There's a reason *healthy* comes before *wealthy* and *wise*.

Though there are no guarantees in life, there *are* certain assurances and things that we can control to help us remain strong and healthy. Diet and exercise are always the best insurance policies, but finances can play a crucial role as well. In this modern era of frugal accounting, if healthcare measures are not provided through employment or by some other means such as Medicare and Medicaid, we need to take into account not only the cost of health insurance, but for out-of-pocket medical expenses as well. Unfortunately, if we happen to be struggling to afford healthcare today, as so many are, these two categories can quickly bankrupt us if we're not careful to manage and control them effectively. Unless we're proactive about our own, as well as our family's personal good health and wellbeing, the medical and insurance industries have a less-than-neighborly habit of putting unhealthy people in the poorhouse.

Despite all the fad diets and fancy workout devices on the market today, undeniably, a sensible diet and simple, moderate exercise is, by far, the best preventive measure one can take to hopefully remain healthy.

As anyone can imagine, during the frontier days, sitting around eating a lot of junk food in front of the television, and not getting enough exercise, was hardly an issue. Back then, most people not only got up with the chickens at the crack of dawn, but also went to bed early, often exhausted from a good-old-fashioned day of hard work while striving to make a wholesome living off the land. The chickens they got up with, along with the eggs produced, were just a vital part of their diet. Life and diets have gotten far more lackadaisical and unhealthier in this day and age.

Nowadays, those who's health insurance is not covered by an employer may find themselves backed into a corner by the healthcare industry, to where they have to carry a high deductible on their medical insurance in order to afford the ever-increasing premiums. Any trips they may have to make to the hospital are a risk of going broke. Unlike the boom or bust of the gold rush days, these days, once bankrupt with medical bills, one cannot easily just pull up stakes, get grubstaked again, and move on to work another claim. Today, medical bills can be devastating.

No, though health insurance and modern medicine didn't exist during the frontier days as it does today, if one was injured or became ill, they wouldn't risk necessarily going broke by seeking medical attention from the town doctor. Some of us may remember old Doc Adams on the television series, Gunsmoke. Healthcare being relatively inexpensive in those times, Doc Adams only took what people could afford, which was oftentimes next to nothing. He wasn't in it for the money as so many are today, especially specialists. The traditional family doctor who once made house calls has become a dying breed from yesteryear.

Today, with single-payer health insurance having such high deductibles, this kind of insurance mostly only provides coverage against catastrophic illnesses and injuries. They're just disaster plans to hopefully keep people from *losing the farm*, so to speak. Additionally, many other medical costs, outside of the deductible, to include hospital outpatient services and copayments, are often considered out-of-pocket expenses by the insurance companies, and may not be routinely covered. Add to that the annual increases in health insurance premiums we've experienced and we're really pushing affordability over a cliff with the healthcare industry having everyone between a rock and a hard place.

The older we get, no matter how healthy we strive to be, unavoidably, the chances of having to use our health insurance increases drastically with time. For example, in my late fifties, though I strived diligently at maintaining my health; in the middle of the night one time, while having a gall-dang-gallbladder attack (as Doc Adams might have described it), I found myself having to admit myself into the hospital emergency room where they had to perform surgery to remove my gallbladder that next morning. That short stint of less than twenty-four hours in the hospital came to nearly thirty thousand dollars, and the insurance initially would only cover about half of it since they considered it short-term, outpatient services. Apparently, you had to be admitted into the hospital for more than just a day to be considered inpatient. All said and done, in addition to my regular insurance premiums, I had to make monthly payments to the hospital for several years to pay off all of those three-hundred-dollar bags of saline solution.

These days, I not only continue to work conscientiously at maintaining my health, but try to budget to keep enough in savings for that rainy day (or middle of the night) to cover any unexpected costs. Unless the laws continue to change in favor of the growing number of people who can no longer afford healthcare, we should remain fearful of having these expenses eat into us even more so in the future.

Having said all that, proper diet and exercise should no longer be an option for any of us, but should be a necessity, unless we want to spend the rest of our lives handing practically everything we have worked so hard for over to the medical and insurance industries.

Of course, we should not forget the legal sector here either, since they contribute to the high costs of healthcare due to malpractice insurance and litigation, which, in effect, is also one of the primary things acting to cripple the medical industry today. Additionally, personal injury and accident lawyers, also known as ambulance chasers are everywhere today. Face it: we live in a sue-happy society these days, where lawyers are coming out of the woodwork to prey upon the systems that we all depend critically upon. Consequently, this medical/insurance/legal trichotomy only acts to feed upon itself and the rest of society.

So how did things ever get this way? Well, looking back in American history, traditionally, many parents have wanted their sons to become doctors or lawyers. The reason being is that becoming a doctor or a lawyer was considered a highly respectable, prestigious, and dignified profession, thereby giving mothers and fathers bragging rights. So, what is it that made doctors and lawyers so respected? You could claim it was because doctors saved lives, and lawyers, well, sometimes saved peoples' behinds. True, that would be an important part of the reasoning. However, let's not fool ourselves; in today's society where money is often valued more than life itself, the *real* reason being a doctor or lawyer is so popular is mainly because they historically have made a lot of money compared to most other professions. Ah, my son the doctor – he not only saves lives, but he's also well off.

Now, in the interest of keep all of those highly valued medical professionals employed successfully, America has gotten so out of shape and overweight that people are at risk of being at the mercy of the healthcare industry. I like to call it the Medical Merry-Go-Round. Today's levels of stress and anxiety aren't helping much either, but proper diet and exercise can go a long way toward keeping those problems under control as well. Provided we eat right and exercise in moderation, no matter what's going on in our lives, things seem to be much more tolerable when we're healthy.

As a society, by choice, we have the ability to control the medical industry, however, as it stands; those with power and wealth continue to dictate the way of life, and death, for everyone else. Currently, far too many people in the healthcare business, including those who manufacture for and market to it, are gaining fortunes at the expense of everyone else. Until we take the excessive profits out of the healthcare industry in general, quality healthcare will never be affordable to the average person, and only the *well-heeled* will be able to afford to become *well-healed*.

I was listening to a conservative talk radio program once when a lady with a very refined southern accent called in to voice her objection to universal healthcare. She expressed what I thought was a very narrow-sided viewpoint in that she didn't want her doctor of choice being pulled away by a socialized healthcare system and kept from fully caring for her personal medical needs. It's safe to assume that she could well afford *her* doctor, although it's getting to where most people can't anymore. Here again, we have a dismal situation where the *haves* don't want to give up what they so adequately have and can easily afford, in order to share it with the *have-nots*. Reading between the lines, she may just as well have come out and said, *who cares about poor people?*

Still, no matter what class of society we may come from, *prevention is the best medicine*, as they say. It can't be stressed enough, when it comes to our health, again, one of the unhealthiest, non-preventive things we Americans do is to center our lives around food and not exercising enough. Ignoring these health risks, the nondiscriminatory killers such as diabetes and cardiovascular disease will catch up to anyone eventually.

Looking around America at present, we often see overweight, out of shape people, driving around the parking lot of stores looking for a place to park as close to the front doors as possible. Sure, the frontier settlers may have hitched their horses and buggies up directly in front of the country mercantile, but then again, they weren't as sedentary as people are today, and didn't need to find ways to exercise so much back then. They also didn't have paved parking lots and pushcarts. Actually, their hard, physical lifestyles could be one of the factors that contributed to putting people in early graves before the age of fifty back then. Today, comparatively, life is much easier.

In the best interest of reducing the skyrocketing costs of healthcare, we all could stand to become more proactive. When we go to the store, as long as we're halfway fit and not genuinely disabled, we should be going out of our way to park in spots farther away from the front doors while leaving the close-in parking spots for the actual handicapped and frail people who really need them. That reminds me of my aunt Jean who once parked in a handicap space and was walking away from her car when a man stopped her and suggested she leave the handicap spaces for the truly handicapped. Well, my aunt, who was known to be somewhat of a character, proceeded to lean down and remove her prosthetic leg, consequently causing the man to eat his words in embarrassment.

For those of us who thankfully don't have prosthetic limbs, and who are fully capable, it wouldn't hurt us to go out of our way to take the stairs instead of the elevator, or go the distance by walking more. We all could stand to be more active. Unfortunately for their health, as well as the cost of healthcare, many Americans have become much less active.

In the State of Colorado, 50% of adults are now either obese or overweight, with children following the same trend, and Colorado is one of the healthiest states in the country. That well correlates with the fact that 50% of the baby boomers in America also now have some form of chronic ailment or disease, most likely cardiovascular disease or diabetes. The way things are going, it probably won't be long before the insurance companies decree that being overweight and out of shape, leading to medical conditions that result from it, such as high blood pressure and hypertension, will be considered preexisting conditions not covered by insurance.

As the phrase goes, *we are what we eat*. If that's the case, America is now a family-sized deluxe pizza with extra cheese, waiting for the doorbell to ring while sitting in recliners fiddling with several remote controls. With advancing technology, it may not be long before people will be sending robots to the door to deal with the pizza guy.

Seriously though, people need to wise up and become far more proactive when it comes to health and safety – their lives depend on it.

Considering ways to stay safe and remain healthy, here's an idea: with many urban neighborhoods being taken over by gangs and drug pushers, perhaps more responsible people could put on safety vests that say *Neighborhood Watch*, then get out and actively walk the neighborhoods for exercise. Not only is it past time for America to gain back its health, it's about time we take back the streets as well. In the process of doing that, we might even get to know other neighbors better than we do now.

I don't mean to be cynical, but too many Americans are guilty of not taking enough responsibility for their own as well as their neighbors health and safety which is driving up the costs of healthcare and public safety for everyone.

So, we all have the need to get moving, safely. When it comes to our health, there's a saying that goes, *when we stop moving, we start dying.* How true that is. Physical, as well as mental activities can therefore be looked upon as being the proverbial fountain of youth. So, if we're interested in not only living longer, but also obtaining freedom from those who enslave us financially, as well as criminally, then we need to get off our duffs and start tackling the risks. In that respect, we should start taking action to stop supporting healthcare services that depend heavily on our undisciplined, unhealthy lifestyles so much. It's simply a matter of choice and self-discipline on our part.

The overall message to everyone concerned should be to shape up, or risk being prematurely shipped out in a pine box, like so many of the frontier people were.

So, here's another method I use personally for staying in shape: when I'm out walking, hiking, or riding my bike, as an added incentive to aid in my exercise, I pretend that there's a ruthless gang of greedy healthcare, insurance, and legal professionals not far behind me. I imagine these scoundrels are trying to catch up to me to beat me up and rob me of my life savings (not all that far from the truth these days). This little exercise works to get me motivated, and gets my cardiovascular system working. Try it sometime. Maybe even get a dog to help you get out on walks more often. Just keep on trucking and don't look back – because they're after you!

Till Life Do Us Part

"How good a society does human nature permit, and, how good a human nature does society permit?"

— Abraham Maslow

So, there we have it, cabins to condos, we have looked back and forth in history and can see clearly where we, as a society, have come from, as well as where we stand currently, but the question remains: what lies ahead?

Here were some interesting projections about how the world and the United States would look in the future as I had noted in the original edition of this book back in 2011. Sources included The Futurist magazine, the United States Census Bureau, and the Bureau of Labor Statistics:

The world will have a billion millionaires by 2025.

By 2023, minorities will comprise more than half of all children in the United States.

The "working age" population of 18–64 is projected to decline to 57% in 2050 from 63% in 2008.

Biobutanol, an advanced biofuel, will outstrip ethanol in popularity.

There will be 1.1 billion vehicles on the world's roads by 2022, up from 800 million.

The number of veterinarians will grow by 35% by 2016, to 84,000.

The number of substance abuse and behavioral disorder counselors will grow by 34% by 2016, to 112,000.

80% of the world's population will have access to electricity by 2030, up from 73% in 2000 and 40% in 1970.

Due to gene therapies, humans will be able to live to the age of 130 by 2030.

The number of people identifying themselves as being of two or more races is projected to more than triple by 2050, to 16.2 million from 5.2 million.

So, how have we been doing? With all the earlier change projections, though our ancestors certainly had their share of challenges, we remain living in a demanding world, but in other ways today that they could have never imagined. Outside of the comforts and conveniences of modern technology, however, I'm not so sure that life is actually improving overall.

Facing priorities, if humanity doesn't begin taking the environment more seriously, will there be any fish left to catch or birds to watch in the future? If the birds and the bees go away, will there be anyone left to love in the world? Back in the early frontier days, these would have been questions that people, at that time, would have not understood much, and would have probably just given blank stares when asked. Today, these same questions have relevance and obvious challenging consequences for the future. However, many people still might give blank stares when asked them. God forbid coffee and chocolate to be in short supply, as predicted, due to climate change and drought – people might then sit up and take notice. Sad as it is, many people today would rather focus on what the stock market is doing rather than what the environment is doing. I'm reminded of a fortune cookie I once opened that said, *"Don't worry about the stock market. Invest in family."* Good advice.

Though history may dictate the past, as well as the present, it doesn't necessarily have to dictate the future. On the contrary, the answers to our problems don't just lie in our history – only our failures. The solutions to our problems lie actually in the present as well as the future with our increasing level of knowledge, experience, technology, and innovation. Education, therefore, has to be the key to an optimal future.

Only through education, will the world wise up and let go of the past. Our future hangs in balance and will only improve through enlightened generations ringing the bells of peace, love, and prosperity. We must therefore teach our children well, so as not to repeat what history has dictated in the past, but what the future beckons going forward. Only the universal force(s) of Nature that created us know that destiny, but as people become more enlightened, we may begin to understand and find true meaning.

Ashes to ashes, dust to dust, eventually all things and beings in the world exchange their natural existence inevitably through the physical realms of animal, mineral, and vegetable. In that regard, theory has it that people and the natural world around them are one in the same, where all physical things and a common energy force between them exist in unison. On a micro level, unless there are destructive cancers present, every cell in the human body communicates and cooperates in harmony (all 50-100 trillion of them). On a more macro level, the same sort of communication and cooperation should be taking place between all people and the planet. In comparison, there's only around eight billion of us people. However, the cancer of egocentricity and ignorance impedes true enlightenment and meaning from happening effectively.

Historically, other cultures, such as the Native Americans, have understood these spiritual principles of Nature best. If those principles are true, then why do we continue to waste our lives fighting among each other if we are, in fact, one in the same, equal parts of Nature itself? If everything in the world and the universe are naturally united, then why should there be any differences between us, including our opinions? Truth is truth. Until we all gain the knowledge and understanding to shed absurdity and realize what absolute truth really is, we will all remain mostly ignorant, though we may each be so absolutely convinced that we are completely right in our own thinking.

So, when will the people of the world finally wise up? Looking around, it may be a while yet before humanity fully gains the level of knowledge and understanding (wisdom) that I'm referring to. Considering the origin of that knowledge, I do believe that we, and everything else made of matter are connected together through a common energy force, and that there has to be much more to this universe than what meets the eye, or that we can ever begin to imagine with our mere mortal minds and basic human senses.

Modern string theory in quantum physics is now discovering that every particle in the universe, through a combined force, appears to display a definite interconnectedness with all other particles of the universe. Sociologically, this would parallel the widely acclaimed concept of a *collective conscience*, or common instinct (common sense), which technically should exist among people, much like the natural instincts that wildlife exhibit. That being the case, there must be an overarching reason and purpose for everyone and everything to be so interconnected.

I feel intuitively that we are all here for higher purpose, for which we as imperfect human beings do not, or cannot possibly have complete knowledge. I also believe that we have been given basic rules to live by, and that these rules should not be taken lightly, especially the underlying guiding principle of love and respect for each other. As I have stated, the prerequisite of loving and respecting others, however, begins with learning to love and respect ourselves first and foremost. I also believe instinctively that there exists another way of life somewhere on the other side of this life, provided we actually learn our lessons while here, and don't get held back somehow to repeat this learning process. With full collective respect and cooperation, rather than competition, we all need to work together to support and help each other to graduate to the next higher level (whatever and wherever that is). God only knows.

Additionally, I feel that we are in a maturing process where knowledge is only being given to us as we become worthy of, and capable of handling it. One way to think about that is this: for the same reason that adults do not allow immature children to play with matches and sharp objects, is why the force(s) of the universe have not yet allowed humanity the technological secrets and knowledge of more powerful things. Such things, like inexhaustible forms of energy to sustain ourselves indefinitely, like nuclear fusion, would probably be extremely dangerous in the wrong hands. As with sharp objects, instead of handling and respecting them as useful tools, we as humans presently would stand to only hurt, if not annihilate ourselves in the process of *mishandling* them. The gift of further elevated levels of higher knowledge and intelligence within our civilization will only come with a more seasoned level of maturity and combined responsibility. It will not be given to us until we reach a point where we can actually and collectively take that responsibility seriously and are fully trustworthy and deserving of it. It surely cannot be entrusted to the greed and corruptness of many of those who are currently in power and control of the world.

Whether we realize it or not, everything, be it good or bad, happens for a reason – that's how we as a society actually grow. Unfortunately, depending on our culture-developed attitudes, there are no guarantees of a perfectly happy existence without problems and challenges. Growing is certainly not always a smooth highway. Bumps and potholes are just a natural part of the process. Fortunately, the road does seem to smooth out with the development of positive attitudes, confidence, optimism, and the power of love and respect. It does that through the individual and combined development of effective human relations principles that involve communication, self-awareness, self-acceptance, self-disclosure, motivation, trust, and of course, conflict resolution.

On the other hand, as I look around, I'm sadly at odds to find a world that is not improving relationships constructively, as it should be. Rather, I see a world that is often in opposition and digressing destructively. Unfortunately, humanity has so far failed at reaching the levels of effective human relations that it is fully and truly capable of reaching.

Faced with our own digression, as the years continue to advance from past to present, into the future, the United States Centers for Disease Control and Prevention (CDC) has disclosed that the suicide rate among Americans has reached a high point. Many of them being war veterans. So, what on Earth could be going on here? Something seriously has gone awry and happened to the very fabric of our society, causing a great deal of anguish and despair.

I suppose life could be losing its meaning to a lot of people due to certain daunting factors found in today's modern society. With so many families being torn apart anymore, perhaps the supporting networks that used to act to promote mental health, and to stem off depression, are losing their grip on us. Just look at the increased usage of prescription antidepressants these days. Another highly related factor that goes along and contributes to that could be our changing cultures, values, and principles. In retrospect, people, as a community, used to care more for each other. Contrarily, the free world today has since transitioned itself into an insanely competitive, self-centered free-for-all. *Do unto others* has been replaced by, *to heck with everyone else, what's in it for me*?

With all of the self-centeredness in the world today, and with so much of it leading to crime, something has to give. That is one of the reasons why I previously took on a higher purpose and challenge of teaching human relations to inmates within the federal prisons, along with becoming a writer. While teaching prisoners who are to be released back into society, my goal was to educate them enough so that they could begin to understand and hopefully start to embrace the concept that to be successful in life, one does not have to focus on gaining either riches, fame, or the acceptance and control of others. Rather, to be successful in life, one must learn to love and respect oneself, while at the same time, genuinely devoting themselves to improving society in one way or another – in service of others. Once people learn and embrace that concept, and put it into practice, the world, in turn, will reward them naturally in ways they cannot imagine.

As the phrase goes, *life is short*, but we all need to learn to live each day to its fullest with positive energy, making it count, unselfishly. What I'm saying is that people have to learn to bask actively in the light of spiritual energy, otherwise known as *love*. So where is the love? Unfortunately, there is a lack of it remaining in many families anymore, let alone outside of family. For example, here is an actual statement from a child (Amy, age six) refusing to complete a school assignment: *"I'm not going to write about the sea – my baby brother is always screaming and being sick, my dad keeps shouting at my mom, and my big sister has just got pregnant, so I can't think what to write."* I believe that could partially explain the underlying cause of the common dysfunction of attention deficit disorder. It's not just that education in this country is failing; it's also a matter of too many families failing. Historically, families were stronger than they are today.

As I first sat writing this book early in the twenty-first century, I looked around and saw a world mostly torn in turmoil. Sadly, there's as much unrest, prejudice, hate, anger, and violence today as there ever has been throughout history, if not more so. In fact, things have gotten so dysfunctional nowadays that many religious people feel that the end days are near, and that the final curtain is destined to come down as predicted in Scriptures. As it stands, many others in this modern world we live in have consequently lost all faith. Looking around and observing current world events, I believe that the end of the world as we know it, has in fact essentially already begun. However, I certainly don't see any point in becoming completely distraught or suicidal over it, though I suspect that some drastic, tough choices and involuntary changes are certainly in store for all of us.

Optimistically, I believe that the true ending of this world ultimately has more to do with the ending of ignorance. This has a lot to do with the progression of education, knowledge, and experience leading finally to a sense of common wisdom and a higher combined intelligence and enlightenment – the modeled concept that I used in teaching human relations that I informally referred to as the *Wise-up Model*. We are now looking, with renewed hope, to younger generations as the most educated ones in our history.

In spite of this, as I've written in the past, one primary situation continues to cause many of the world's problems, and that is arrogant, egotistical values, blinded by competitive greed and corruption, widely intensified by false cultures, often under the influence of drugs and alcohol. With drugs, the most influential of them being naturally or artificially produced hormones. What's frightening is that the pharmaceutical companies are now heavily pushing male-enhancing testosterone boosters, as if we don't have enough problems revolving around these hormones as it is.

In relation to hormones and the education of young people, why do you think so many schools are trending away from coed environments? The reason being, non-coed environments without all of the primitive gender distractions are far more conducive to the actual process of education and the instilling of knowledge in our young people. Coed schooling, all-too-often, gives way to more of a *social scene* where education takes a back seat to socializing and extracurricular activities. Consequently, our traditional public-school systems, while mostly under the control of politicians, administrators, and unions, have become mostly a waste of taxpayer dollars. They've become more of a professional daycare environment and source of professional entitlement, often centered on social and financial gains, rather than serious education. Just look at what happened with Penn State, among other colleges, putting football at the top of its values, ahead of its true purpose in education.

At present, especially when dealing with poverty situations, improperly educated kids that never mature intellectually, tend to evolve into less-than-intelligent grown people who only act to further procreate others like themselves, and the beat goes on with this chain never being broken. In other words, dysfunctional families, along with dysfunctional education systems, tend to lead to only more societal dysfunction. Consequently, only 9 out of 100 students living in poverty in this country graduate from college.

There are, however, certain bright spots beginning to develop in America, such as in the state of Iowa, where serious reforms in the right direction are being made to the educational systems there. Other than these bright spots, the main concern is that our society continues to focus on all the wrong things, distracted away from truly effective education while the rest of the world passes us by and overtakes us competitively.

We seem to be more focused on extreme forms of entertainment, to include competitive violence that takes place in stadiums and arenas, delivered over scores of cable and satellite channels, viewed on big-screen TVs. Like the obsession with the gladiators of the past Roman Empire, people can't seem to get enough of it. If not for the demand for extreme forms of entertainment and the fame and fortunes that result from that demand, for what true purpose do people need to watch competitive violence anyway? Out of all this senseless entertainment, there's a growing number of professional athletes, many of whom have stooped to using Human Growth Hormones in order to compete for multimillion-dollar contracts. One high-profile athlete actually went so far as to say he did it to feed his family. What was he feeding them, caviar?

Apparently, in the Middle East, entertainment technology, coupled with competitive violence, hasn't quite caught up to America yet, so radical, extreme young people pass their time by blowing themselves up in the midst of innocent bystanders. How intelligent is that?

Observing all of this dysfunction, we have to ask: where is the true value-based parenting and education? As for the misled male gender, we can keep claiming *boys will be boys*; however, society should come to its senses and no longer buy into that lame excuse anymore. Fact of the matter is, boys, under the influence of peer pressure, drugs and alcohol, hormones, and the media will become whoever poor parenting, bad education, and cultural brainwashing brought them up to be. Proper, responsible parenting and effective education are the only things that will ever turn things around. Otherwise, the end of the world, as the doomsayers claim, could in fact be near, where we stand to become the victims of each other. Though the means to that end may have already begun, if we as a society don't *wise-up* and start respecting each other and the environment, natural forces may step in and take control with all of its furry and power, wiping the slate clean while restoring natural order.

Therefore, I have come to realize, even though we have been hit over the head with it all our lives, for generations, and continue to resist it, that the ultimate lesson that we are all here on Earth to learn is to love genuinely, and respect everything and everyone around us. The underlying problem that I will continue to stress, however, is that we first and foremost, as a prerequisite of that level of human relations, must learn primarily to love and respect *ourselves* before we can ever possibly love and respect anyone or anything else in the world. Thus, we have the very paradox that society just can't seem to overcome and rise above. Many people, due to their dysfunctional backgrounds or non-positive life experiences and attitudes, may be highly challenged in the ability to love and respect anything, let alone themselves.

Awareness and change are often stimulated auspiciously through suffering and pain, be it mental and/or physical, and since we're all imperfect beings, we are all therefore subjected to this grief to a degree necessary for us actually to change. With that, I feel that suffering and pain is not inflicted upon us merely to punish us, but rather necessarily to enlighten us. Moreover, we need to keep in mind that in the end, suffering and pain may be a miniscule price to pay for what we truly stand to gain. Crisis and the suffering it can cause is therefore merely the systematic catalyst that facilitates the ability and willingness for people to change toward what we were created and are truly meant to be – loving, cooperative people.

The other prerequisite for the ability to love both others and ourselves is unconditional forgiveness, again starting with ourselves. It is imperative that we be able to forgive ourselves before we can ever begin to forgive anyone else. None of the above worthwhile can be accomplished otherwise.

Of course, there are circumstances where people go blindly through life carelessly and obliviously disrespecting everyone, including themselves, to which may give a fully justified reason for reincarnation, as well as the continuing of suffering and pain. Considering a scientific principle, for every action, there is an equal and opposite reaction. In that regard, all the pain and suffering one causes others in this life, they may come to experience in the next. Therefore, lessons not learned in this life may necessarily have to be repeated in the next. Thus, we have the true reasons and the legitimate need for reincarnation, a concept that many people cannot seem to grasp and accept mostly due to religious indoctrination.

As I have well indicated throughout this book, I feel strongly that extreme competition, although highly valued historically and currently in our society, is not necessarily good for society. Extreme competition often has a terrible result of instilling self-centeredness in people to where they can become obsessed with winning over others, paramount to anything else they might value. Instead of obsessing over beating others to the punch, or across the finish line, we should all be unselfishly serving others less fortunate than ourselves to succeed along with us in cooperation, not so much in competition.

With all this in mind, I believe it's past time to cure the uncooperative cancer that is killing our society. Rather, we should transform the '*No Child Left Behind*' concept to the next level so that no one, child *or* adult is left behind. United States, United Kingdom, United Nations, United World. United everything and everyone. The key word here being *united*, solving not only local and regional problems, but also world problems. That said, we, meaning people as well as countries, should first and foremost be solving our biggest problems *together*, such as climate change and global warming, through cooperation, rather than extreme competition. Ideally, wars should never exist and militaries should only be National and World guards instead. As has been said, if we can visualize it, it can be done. This idealism simply has not been allowed in the past, but if the world is to survive, it must be allowed for the future.

~

In conclusion, if I haven't at least to some degree enlightened anyone who had the patience, as well as the interest to read this book in its entirety, then I suppose I haven't accomplished much, but I trust that is not the case or you wouldn't be reading these very words at this moment.

More than anything, however, I wish for the combined success in finding our way across the cobblestones and through the cobwebs of life – collectively. We just need to remember, along the way, that we are all in this together for a reason. Somehow, in the end, I believe firmly that all the turmoil, toil, suffering and pain to get there will be finally realized and understood with true wisdom and enlightenment – the final destination being well worth the long, bitter journey. In the meantime, we should not forget an important aspect of life: that is to take full individual responsibility for our actions, and respect the rights of others as much as we should respect ourselves. Moreover, we should strive to live, learn, laugh, and above all, embrace the most important fundamentals of life itself, to experience PEACE, LOVE, and JOY.

Cabins to condos, life ever after, void of suffering and pain, full of peace, love, and joy, I believe is truly meant to be the final frontier.